'In *Closing Ranks*, Leroy Logan takes you on a personal journey to the Caribbean, where you are introduced to his parents. They are two ordinary people of Jamaican heritage with an extra-ordinary ambition – to travel to Britain, to contribute to the rebuilding of the country after the war, and to improve the lives of their future family. On arrival, they are met with hostility, but perseverance and resilience win the day, often at great cost.

Leroy, this son of immigrants, is equally ambitious – a man with goals of his own, determined to forge his own path. Through a "Damascus road" experience, he soon learns to depend on God, expressing deep appreciation as he identifies "the hand of God" at work in his life. This gives him the tremendous courage needed to stand firm against the institutional racism he encounters within the Metropolitan Police.

This autobiography highlights the significance of self-belief and the importance of service to the community. It reveals a deep desire to make a difference, a strong commitment to family and faith, and a determination to model the changes one wishes to see. Plain speaking in describing the highs and lows of being an "outstanding" member of the Met, Leroy is not afraid to share his vulnerability, and you can feel the pride with which he receives a variety of accolades. An impossible journey has been made possible by faith! Leroy Logan is a great example of achievement against all the odds.'

The Rt Revd Rose Hudson-Wilkin, Bishop of Dover

'I have known Leroy for many years and have always been impressed with his ability to look at issues from different angles, to work in partnership with others and not to be afraid of making tough decisions. This timely book is a must for anyone who has a heart for justice in our society, offering a deeper understanding of the issues and hope for a better tomorrow.'

Patrick Regan OBE, CEO of Kintsugi Hope

An acknowledgement

'When I first met Leroy Logan in the mid-1970s, little did I know our paths would cross twenty-five years later through the tragic circumstances around the murder of my son Damilola. Notwithstanding that we were related through his marriage to my cousin Gretl in the early 1980s, I felt reassured that his immense experience in community policing and his genuine desire to build bridges with all sections of the public would have a significant impact in the investigation, and it did.

Therefore, when I was asked to write a recommendation for his book I did so unreservedly because of my genuine admiration for him. Not only in surviving thirty years in the MPS, but also in retirement the last seven years where he still stands up against inequalities and injustices in society, repeatedly giving of his time to grassroots organizations like my charity in the name of my son, the Damilola Taylor Trust. I look forward to working with him in the run-up to the twentieth anniversary of Damilola's death in November 2020.'

Richard Taylor OBE

Born in 1957 to Jamaican parents, Leroy Logan is a proud Londoner, a staunch Arsenal fan, an advocate for good relationships between the police and Britain's minority ethnic communities, a mentor to young people, and an advisor on knife crime and social justice.

Co-author George Luke is a writer, journalist and award-winning radio producer. He has interviewed politicians, pop stars, authors, activists and intellectuals, and particularly enjoys profiling people who have made a notable contribution to the world. George has contributed to several books including *The Rough Guide to World Music and The Rough Guide to Rock.*

CLOSING RANKS

My life as a cop

Leroy Logan MBE
with George Luke

Originally published in hardback in Great Britain in 2020

Society for Promoting Christian Knowledge
36 Causton Street
London SW1P 4ST
www.spck.org.uk

Reprinted four times
Reissued in paperback 2021
Copyright © Leroy Logan and George Luke 2020, 2021

British Library Cataloguing-in-Publication Data
A catalogue record for this book is available from the British Library

ISBN 978-0-281-08347-3
eBook ISBN 978-0-281-08348-0

1 3 5 7 9 10 8 6 4 2

Typeset by Nord Compo
First printed in Great Britain by Jellyfish Print Solutions
Subsequently digitally printed in Great Britain

eBook by Nord Compo

Produced on paper from sustainable forests

Contents

Illustrations

List of illustrations

Foreword

I first met Leroy when I was researching stories about the West Indian experience for my BBC project SMALL AXE, a collection of films about the real lives of extraordinary West Indians living in London from the late 60s to the early 80s – a time of struggle with the authorities, for cultural identity and recognition. I was interested in stories about remarkable people or events which I felt had been ignored, or swept under the carpet.

Leroy's story was at once both ordinary and unique: an ordinary man, who made the best of everything for himself – whether it was in his education or his determination in sticking with the police force; even his immaculate appearance told me a story.

For a West Indian man to join the police force in the early 80s, at the time of the Brixton uprisings, and stick with it in the way Leroy did, is unique. I was amazed and intrigued by the way he had stood his ground and progressed within the Metropolitan Police against so many obstacles: hostility, outright racism and being repeatedly overlooked for promotion. What interested me the most was his way of joining the force even though his father had recently been badly beaten up by two police officers. What kind of man was he?

Steve McQueen
May 2020

Prologue:
When two worlds collide

Sometimes your worst nightmare can be your biggest breakthrough.

In 1982, I was in my comfort zone. My first love was science, and I had secured a place in one of the most eminent teaching hospitals in the world, headed by a world-renowned gastroenterologist. CV-wise, I was set for a career in science. And then all of a sudden, the call of policing hit. It took me completely out of my comfort zone – and in all honesty, it was my worst nightmare.

In signing up for the Metropolitan Police, I would be joining an organization I had no love for. I was the victim of the Sus laws growing up; I'd seen the way police officers treated people who looked like me, and it was sickening. And yet I sensed that there was a purpose for me in the Met, even though I knew that joining would set two worlds – my personal life and my professional life – on a collision course.

Those two worlds started colliding before I'd even put a police uniform on, when two officers viciously assaulted my father shortly after I submitted my application to join the Met. They would collide again and again over the years that followed. But I never once imagined that they would collide in such a dramatic way as they did with the murder of Damilola Taylor in the autumn of 2000.

I first encountered the Taylor family in the early 1970s when my wife Gretl and I were dating. Damilola's father, Richard, is a cousin of Gretl's; I would often see him and his then girlfriend,

Gloria, at various family events Gretl took me to. We were all in our twenties back then. Unfortunately, we lost touch after Richard and Gloria got married and returned to Nigeria to raise their family.

I didn't instantly make the connection when the tragic story of Damilola's murder hit the headlines in November 2000. I can still recall the CCTV footage capturing the last moments of his life, as he skipped innocently from the library on his way home to the North Peckham Estate. Those vivid images touched my heart, both as a parent and as a police officer. A murder investigation (code name Operation Seale) was launched shortly afterwards, but I quickly gathered from reliable internal sources that it wasn't making much progress.

Given the Black Police Association's (BPA's) ethos of being a bridge between the police and the black community, I felt that it was only right for me to represent the Association – as chair – at a memorial service held for Damilola shortly after his murder. I immediately felt at home as I entered the Pentecostal church on the Old Kent Road – especially when I caught sight of Gretl's nephew, Kehinde Ogundipe, sitting on the front row. We greeted each other, and in a jaw-dropping moment, Kehinde confirmed that Damilola was family: he was Richard and Gloria's son.

Commander Joe Kay, the lead officer on Operation Seale, approached me after the service. Our conversation was brief but positive, and I wasn't totally surprised when he invited me to join the Gold Group overseeing the investigation. Gold Groups are part of the legacy of the Macpherson Inquiry, which followed the racist murder of Stephen Lawrence in 1993. The Met defines a Gold Group as 'a strategic forum designed to add value to the response to an internal or external Critical Incident'. This one consisted of senior representatives from the Homicide Investigation Team, the local police and emergency services, officials from Southwark Council and some other members of the community who had a significant advocacy role.

Althea Smith, a prominent councillor in the borough of Southwark, encouraged me to join the Gold Group. Both she and Joe Kay helped me overcome my initial apprehension at joining. I knew the investigation team wouldn't embrace me with open arms, and I felt strongly that the people I was supposed to be working with would close ranks against me and shut me out. My perception was confirmed right before my first meeting with them, when I heard through the operational grapevine ('Rumour Control', as we called it) that the investigation team saw me as a threat.

Knowing this, I approached that first meeting with, at the forefront of my mind, the objective of reassuring the investigation team that I wasn't going to be a threat. I was careful to acknowledge their expertise and experience while making it known that my role was to assist in filling any gaps. I was there to be part of the solution, not to create barriers. I sensed that if I worked it right, my actions would be an advantage for this and future investigations involving communities that lacked trust and confidence in the police. I wasn't going to make my family connection with the Taylors known at this stage, since I didn't know how my colleagues would have perceived this. Nevertheless, I felt I was in this position for a reason.

At that first meeting, Commander Kay and the community representatives gave me a warm welcome – in complete contrast to the suspicious looks I got from the investigation team and local borough officers. I could understand their position; my attendance was uncharted territory for all of us. I maintained a quiet focus throughout that meeting, absorbing all the information from the different representatives. As I did so, I felt the burden of responsibility that the public outcry for a breakthrough had placed on each of them.

What brought a tear to my eye was the detailed account of how Damilola's innocent life had collided with the hardened street culture of the local youths who regularly created fear and intimidation in the North Peckham Estate area. Naively, Damilola had stood his ground and wouldn't be intimidated by them, having recently arrived from Nigeria and believing he should stand up for himself. Some would say he wasn't sufficiently street-savvy for urban London life and was more used to the Lagos culture, where people stood up for themselves without the risk of life-threatening retribution.

Young Damilola was isolated and surrounded by the mob one winter evening in a deserted part of the estate on his way home from the library. Tragically he was subject to an unprovoked attack and was stabbed in the leg. He was able to break free, but unfortunately as he tried to run back home, he lost enormous amounts of blood with every stride and he collapsed in a dimly lit stairwell. By the time emergency services attended the scene, they were unable to save him because of the excessive loss of blood.

Two things came across very strongly in that meeting: the collective determination of the group to catch the perpetrators, and the utter frustration they felt at the lack of significant intelligence they'd gathered, despite repeated house-to-house enquiries. Some of the residents of houses that looked right onto the area where Damilola was stabbed were not even opening their doors to the investigation team, for fear of retribution from the local thugs suspected of the murder.

This 'wall of silence', as the media and the community representatives described it, was discussed extensively at that first Gold Group meeting – and again at another meeting a few days later. At the second meeting, Althea Smith made a radical request for black officers to assist with the house-to-house enquiries. I could see the horrified looks on some of my colleagues' faces, while the other community representatives nodded in agreement. Althea backed her request up with her experience in the area. She knew that people there had a greater affinity with officers they shared a cultural similarity with – be that their ethnicity, language, shared history – or some other common experience. Invariably, these would overcome any reluctance they might have had, despite any past experiences of heavy-handed policing they had suffered.

My colleagues appeared outraged by such a suggestion. Meanwhile, I had to hold myself back from nodding furiously in agreement. Althea's comments reflected a report I had submitted on this issue a couple of years earlier to Deputy Assistant Commissioner Bill Griffiths, the head of the CID Training School at Hendon, during the roll-out of the Macpherson Inquiry recommendations in 1999. I saw this as an opportunity to show the advantages of this previously untested model of policing (known to me as 'Affinity Policing') in a high profile investigation.

I told the group how whenever I encountered someone of African-Caribbean origin, they would talk to me in their native tongue or some form of Creole. Even though I would not immediately understand what they were saying, I realized they felt more comfortable with me than with my white counterparts. This was in total contrast to when I joined the Met in the early 1980s, when communicating with the public in languages other than English was frowned upon. If a white colleague caught you doing so, he or she would indicate, verbally or by gestures, that it was a no-no. Black and minority ethnic officers, however, quickly recognized the importance of communicating with the public at all levels and in as many languages as possible, and the benefits this brought to our work. Unfortunately, some of our white counterparts failed to recognize – or would simply never acknowledge – these benefits, despite the empirical evidence

and objective business cases that have proven it, in both public and private organizations. I knew from very early on that a
more reflective organization, using its languages and cultural
intelligence in an operational setting, would be a great asset. I
now had a chance to prove it.

After extensive debate for and against Althea's suggestion,
Commander Kay asked me to form a squad of officers that mir-
rored the local African-Caribbean community, to carry out the
next wave of house-to-house enquiries. When I reported this
back to the BPA executive, not only did they give it a unani-
mous vote of confidence, they also volunteered to help select
the team members. We soon had a shortlist of 20 officers from
our membership database. Within a couple of days, we had a
squad leader: Sergeant Paul Martin, a rising star known for his
leadership skills in the south-west London section of the Met.
Later that week, Paul submitted a dream team of nine officers,
including three women: Deborah Akinlawon, Janet Barracks
and Sabinah Johnson.

I made a strategic decision to keep the group at arm's length
to make their integration into the Operation Seale investigation team seamless, relying on Paul to keep me informed of
their development. Nothing could have prepared me for the
dramatic impact they would have within hours of their deployment. It was with great anticipation that I attended their initial debriefing sessions; they never failed to amaze me each
time they shared their achievements. I observed how they drew
together as a cohesive and dynamic team. I wasn't surprised
when within a few days, they had given themselves a name: the
Cultural Resource Unit (CRU).

An example of the CRU's immediate impact was the experience of two officers, Deborah Akinlawon and Jimi Tele. During
their first wave of house-to-house enquiries, they went to homes
where repeated visits by white officers had not even elicited a

response from the occupants. When they went, they had the presence of mind to shout through the letterbox, 'Auntie (or 'Uncle') it's me' in Yoruba, a Nigerian language predominantly spoken in the southern regions of the country, especially in Lagos, the capital. From within the veil of silence would come the cautious voice of an occupant saying, 'Ah – you're Nigerian?' to which they would respond, 'Yes, Uncle' or 'Yes, Auntie' (in Nigeria and many other African countries, addressing an older person as 'Uncle' or 'Auntie' is seen as a mark of respect). This would be promptly followed by the unbolting of a secured door and the occupant gesticulating anxiously for them to enter the premises quickly. Within a couple of hours, Debbie and Jimi would emerge with critical intelligence for the investigation. Affinity Policing was already proving its worth.

It was essential that I was fully objective on the CRU's performance, so I left it to Operation Seale's supervisors to assess the team's outcomes. Their summary report was very complimentary. It noted, among other things, that within the first few days of their deployment, the CRU had gathered potentially important intelligence and passed it on to the enquiry team, thanks to people's willingness to speak to them. The only negative feedback they'd had was members of the community saying, 'Why has it taken so long for you to arrive? You should have been here the day after it happened!'

Thanks to the quality of intelligence gathered in such a short time, the CRU was asked to carry out other important actions and allocated vehicles to do so. This gave it a level of unforeseen kudos and respect, and facilitated its seamless integration into the Homicide Investigation Team. The CRU officers grew exponentially in confidence and in their investigative abilities. I saw an appetite for complex investigations that had been lying dormant in them surface fully, as newly found skills and abilities blossomed. They did not always see eye to eye, but in the majority of issues they coalesced, exhibiting a can-do attitude to overcome any challenges they faced.

At subsequent Gold Group meetings, I was more than pleased to report our amazing impact. My great sense of relief was outshone by my overwhelming sense of pride. To get such immediate results despite the inherent risks vindicated my total confidence in the CRU officers. I was pleasantly surprised that the scepticism my colleagues initially had was quickly replaced by a more positive – if somewhat grudging – tone of support. They never explicitly vocalized their support in my presence or in the meeting minutes; instead, they implicitly conceded defeat in their general disposition towards the CRU and me. Over the subsequent weeks and months, I wasn't surprised to see many of them owning these breakthroughs in the investigation. Success has many guardians; failure is an orphan.

It was a huge burden removed for all concerned when two suspects were charged. It had extra meaning for Gloria and Richard as a part of their closure process, but it was also poignant for the local community to know that some of the youngsters who frequently terrorized them were off the streets or under close investigation. There was total agreement in the Gold Group meeting that the CRU's culturally relevant investigatory practices had a dramatic impact that precipitated the identification of the suspects.

Unfortunately, the press releases and interviews made by key Met spokespersons on behalf of the Southwark Borough officers and the Homicide Team failed to fully acknowledge the unit that made such a difference. It would have been reasonable for Paul Martin to be interviewed – or even just mentioned – for his role as the CRU's leader, but this never happened. This oversight was repeated in Bishop John Sentamu's review of Operation Seale. I wrote him a three-page letter raising my observations, but he never responded – not then, nor in subsequent meetings at which I reminded him of the letter. Nevertheless, the report showed that the Met had learned many lessons from the Macpherson Inquiry recommendations, and that the mistakes made following the racist murder of Stephen Lawrence were not repeated.

Sadly, things did not go totally as planned. The boys who were charged were not convicted because the main witness was not reliable. Despite this, nobody on the team gave up in their efforts to see justice served. At a subsequent trial, the suspects were convicted, based on more reliable forensic evidence from the murder scene, found on their clothing.

All throughout the case, my professional and personal involvement clashed, stretching me emotionally and spiritually. The senior investigating officer on the case assigned a Family Liaison Officer (FLO) to be the communication bridge between the Taylor family and the Homicide Team. I had to keep my family connections private while reassuring the family that the investigation was progressing – and I had to do so without compromising the FLO'S role. If I got it wrong, I could cause unnecessary conflict between the investigation team and the family. This would have been the last thing anyone wanted, especially with the gaze of the national and international media on us.

The pump priming of the investigation by the CRU drew on a greater sense of pride from the community members on the Gold Group, especially Althea Smith. She even went out on patrol with us to see Affinity Policing in action. The positive interactions between the CRU and the local youngsters showed diversity in action, culminating in them nicknaming the officers their 'Black Squad' – which brought an extra glow to Althea's smile.

Having seen evidence that it could work, I was determined to develop the equivalent of the CRU across the Met, with a clear link to the legacy of Damilola's short life and what he stood for, fully owned by his parents. I put together a strong business case which I submitted to DAC Bill Griffiths – which, in turn, reminded him of the Affinity Policing concept report I had sent to him a couple of years earlier. Consequently, we had a meeting where he fully embraced the concept and acknowledged his past oversight.

Bill took total ownership by agreeing to chair the CRU programme board I proposed in the business case. Having such an extremely senior ambassador opened doors and drew on the cooperation of the right people to make the CRU concept a reality. This began with Specialist Operations totally owning the CRU and fully resourcing it with a fully competent backup team in a well-resourced office, the creation of a secure database made up of police personnel vetted for their abilities, qualifications and skills – personal and professional – that could be of assistance in the investigation of serious and major crimes, and the selection of senior officers for on-call duties as CRU coordinators. It was great to make up the first cohort of coordinators.

All of this gave the CRU automatic credibility as an integral part of the world-renowned Specialist Operations, especially after the soft internal launch of the CRU office and trained coordinators in November 2002, followed by its official launch at Scotland Yard in February 2004 with Gloria and Richard as special guests. I ensured that the officers who made up the original CRU were given the credit they deserved, to address the wrong of being overlooked when they were part of Operation Seale.

Gloria and Richard continued to give the CRU and me regular moments of appreciation in the early years of developing the Damilola Taylor Trust. But the ultimate offer of appreciation was the level of prominence the family gave them at Damilola's funeral, held in January 2001. I worked closely with Bill Griffiths, assisting him with interpreting the cultural emphasis of a

Nigerian funeral in a church setting, and ensuring that the Met was shown at its appropriate best under the gaze of the international media. I felt privileged to represent the CRU and the Met at the memorial services and subsequent anniversary events.

As one of the on-call CRU coordinators, I was regularly on standby waiting for calls from senior investigating officers working on murders, kidnappings and hostage sieges. As time passed, I was able to show the Met that my family connections to the Taylors had not had a detrimental impact on my professional conduct, to ensure I had a positive impact on the investigation.

It saddened me greatly when a cost-saving review of the CRU's performance relegated it to HR Logistics, which automatically reduced its specialist kudos and consigned it to bureaucratic obscurity. This sent a strong signal to many of the Met's minority ethnic staff – especially those on the CRU-protected database – that the added value of diversity in a more reflective organization was not a priority.

It appears to me that this lack of emphasis on diversity continues today, and is preventing the Met from being fully reflective of London. It is making improvements in terms of gender issues and quite rightly so, but it is not as successful in terms of officers from minority ethnic communities joining the organization and staying to complete their 30 years. This lack of emphasis ties in with the shelving of key performance indicators on recruiting, retention and progression of minority ethnic officers, as instructed by the Macpherson Inquiry. It is ironic that the scrapping of these indicators had a direct influence on the CRU – one of the direct outcomes from another high-profile killing of a young black male, Stephen Lawrence.

I also felt led to support the DTT (Damilola Taylor Trust) events and build a friendship with the CEO, Gary Trowsdale. He was the main driving force behind one of the DTT offshoots, the highly acclaimed Spirit Of London Awards in the early to mid-2000s for talented young movers and shakers in London. It didn't end there: the awards alumni formed the 1BC (One Big Community) initiative to build a platform for young people to speak truth to power under Gary's guidance supported by me until 2016, followed by the cross-political party Youth Violence Commission, which reported in 2018 and 2020. The journey continues!

Damilola, God bless your soul and rest in eternal peace. Your legacy to change the world lives on.

1

From Islington
to Spanish Town – and back

'Don't ever tell me that you're bored, because if you do, I will give you something to do.'

You know you're officially a parent when you hear the words your parents used, to instil discipline or chastise you, coming out of your mouth directed at your offspring. Even as I said those words to my firstborn son, Gerad, for the first time (and again to him and his younger siblings several times over the years as they were growing up), I would hear my dad's voice saying them to me when I was a youngster. You could put my being a disciplinarian down to having been a police officer for 30 years, but it really began with my dad's influence on me. 'Idle hands are the devil's weapon,' Dad would always say. 'Keep yourself busy.'

Neither of my parents were on the *Empire Windrush*'s historic voyage from Kingston to Tilbury in 1948; nevertheless, they were very much part of what we now call 'The Windrush Generation'. Oswald Kenneth Logan and Daphne Pearl Goldburn met in Salt River, a small town in the Clarendon parish in the south of Jamaica. My dad worked for Monymusk, the rum distillery and sugar refinery that is a huge part of Clarendon's economy. Dad was a handsome guy; always stylish and well-dressed, he had quite a lot of female admirers. Mum, on the other hand, wasn't into dressing in the latest fashions or having a flamboyant wardrobe. She certainly knew how to dress (she was a dressmaker, after all), but she preferred to keep a low profile. She was a quiet, steady, loving woman. You wouldn't have imagined the two of them as a match because of the differing ways they presented themselves, but somehow they worked as a couple. Opposites can sometimes attract and forge fulfilling long-term relationships.

Dad made the journey over to the UK on his own. The common practice among people emigrating from the Caribbean in those days was that the man would set out first, find his feet and secure a job, and then send for his wife or future partner to join him once he had settled. There's something biblical about it; that image of the groom going off to 'prepare a place' for his bride to come and live with him. That's what Dad did in 1954, and in 1955 he booked a boat ticket for Mum to come and join him in England. They got married in 1956; I arrived the following year.

Dad was very strongly steeped in the Jamaican culture that held the Queen, the Commonwealth and the British government in great reverence. He had a lot of relatives and friends who had fought in the Second World War, but he hadn't gone to war himself because he was too young when the war was on. However, he did grow up with that strong sense of Britain being the 'Mother Country', and a good knowledge of how Jamaica had served the Mother Country in the fight against Hitler. On arriving in Britain, he was shocked to discover that the respect people in the Caribbean had for Britain wasn't reciprocated, and that the generation of brave Caribbean men and women who had fought for the Mother Country had all gone from hero status to zero status. They would go looking for accommodation, only to be greeted by signs saying, 'No Irish, no blacks, no dogs.' They couldn't get bank loans. They had to host rent parties in order to afford the rent on their rooms. Some of them were really stuck and finding it tough surviving the hostile environment.

I was born in Islington, and my earliest memories are of growing up around Caledonian Road when I was three. We lived in Thornhill Square. It's a very wealthy area now, sometimes used as a location for film shoots. Dad was an incredibly hard worker, and he had an entrepreneurial side to him. He teamed up with some friends, who had also made the trip over from Jamaica, with a vision of getting into the property market. Unfortunately, his partners in that venture defrauded him, cutting him out of the house they'd teamed up to buy together. He found this really hard to take – especially given that they had all grown up together back in Jamaica. He tried to sue them, but that didn't work as he couldn't afford a lawyer. In the end, he decided not to take the law into his own hands. He was a great believer in the principle that you reap what you sow.

Mum was a very gifted dressmaker. Whenever I was on holiday from school, I would be in whichever factory she happened to be working in. She would either be making dresses or ironing them. As time went on, she had problems with her eyesight and her fingers were not as nimble as they used to be, and so she did more of the ironing than the dressmaking. But whether she was making dresses or ironing them, she loved the atmosphere in the factories. Dad worked in a plastic moulding factory for a while, but it started to affect his hands and so he gave it up and became a long-distance lorry driver.

After a few years of London life, Mum got very homesick and decided to go back to Jamaica with my sister Hyacinth and me. I was five and Hyacinth was just a few months old. We sailed from Tilbury Docks to Jamaica on a Spanish boat – a right old tin pan. Even at the age of five, I knew that this was not luxury travel! But Mum hated flying, so the tin pan was our only option. The voyage took about three weeks, with tempestuous storms throughout. I got really ill the first week, but we arrived in Jamaica safe and sound. We lived in an area called Tredegar

Park, on the outskirts of Spanish Town. It was a bit of a shanty-town, but the compound we lived in was vibrant and new. All the folks nearby were taken with my London accent, and they would pay me to speak just so that they could hear it. I really capitalized on that. They all seemed to believe that I was going to be a pastor. They nicknamed me 'Deacon', and I would hold church services in the compound, preaching my heart out until Mum called me in for dinner.

The Rio Grande wasn't that far from where we lived, and we used to go and bathe there. It got its name from the days the Spanish ruled Jamaica, back in the fifteenth and sixteenth centuries, and it's a very rough river with rapids – a popular destination for people who enjoy whitewater rafting and kayaking. But it also has a lot of natural pools, and these were where we would go and wash. Mum was always warning me to steer clear of the rapids, but one day I slipped and got caught in them. I couldn't swim very well, and it wasn't long before I was totally immersed in white water. I didn't hit any of the rocks, but not being a strong swimmer, I immediately thought that this was it. Just then, I had an out-of-body experience. I looked down and I could see myself in slow motion – being twirled round and round as if I were in a washing machine.

To this day, I don't know where my cousin Bobby came from or how he got to me. But just as I was thinking to myself that this was the end, I felt him grab me and pull me up out of the water. My spirit and my body came back together with a thump. I gasped a lungful of air, looked at him and said, 'Bobby, where did you come from?'

I came out of that river with the sense that a guardian angel was watching over me. Since then, one of my favourite Bible verses has been Psalm 37:23 – 'The Lord makes firm the steps of the one who delights in him.' I've always remained beholden to Bobby for saving my life. He was an aspiring golfer, and his story was similar to Seve Ballesteros. Seve learned to play golf using branches from trees, and Bobby was exactly the same. He learned his trade being a caddy for all the American golfers who came over to Jamaica. Eventually he moved to the USA, but he didn't make the big time. I wonder why?

What my parents hadn't realized when we set sail for Jamaica was that Mum was pregnant with her third child. Shortly after I started school, she gave birth to a little boy, O'Neil. Unfortunately, she had some complications during the birth and had to stay in hospital for a few weeks. O'Neil was sent to stay with our aunt while Mum was kept in the hospital; sadly, he died after a few weeks. It was devastating to all of us, even though we'd only known him for two weeks. It was doubly devastating for Dad, because he was on the other side of the world when it happened, and he didn't even have a photograph of his baby son. To this day, we wonder what life would have been like with O'Neil in the family.

Losing O'Neil made Mum decide she wanted to return to England. But it was another three years before we made the journey back in 1966 – arriving in time for me to see England win the World Cup.

***

I'd really missed my dad while we were in Jamaica, so I was glad we were all together again. Mum was glad to be back too, but was still suffering from the stress of losing O'Neil, which hit her hard psychologically. She was already going through a lot of mental health issues; she had been diagnosed as schizophrenic, and for many years she suffered with hallucinations. She was obviously upset over what had happened, but she didn't hold any animosity towards the doctors. All through those times, I saw Dad constantly offer her his support, caring for her, and I would fill in for him when he was at work. This meant I couldn't always play out when I wanted, because my responsibilities at home and to mum came first. As a first-generation British Jamaican, I fully took on my carer responsibilities without any reservations, mirroring what I had observed in Jamaica. Unlike today, it wasn't even recognized, much less acknowledged, by the health services. It was 20-odd years after her diagnosis that the doctors realized that she hadn't been made aware that she should not have any dairy products with the medication she was on. Once she cut dairy products from her diet, she was fine.

Mum was the quiet one; always stable, echoing whatever Dad would say. She was the prayer warrior in the family; her faith was unshakeable. Mum was quite strong; loving but stern – a nice balance between getting us to do things and to do as we were told. She was very God-fearing; always singing hymns and quoting the Bible. Mum knew she had an anchor, and she could get through her troubles. She smoked like a chimney. Dad used to smoke a pipe. Harold Wilson was still very prominent back then and he smoked a pipe, and it gave my dad that sort of stately politician appearance, watching him smoke his pipe and read his paper. When Dad was reading his paper, we just left him alone. Faith-wise, Dad was like Mum, but without the hymn-singing and Bible-quoting. He was clear on his principles. They both went to the local Baptist church from time to time. I always felt clear where my sense of purpose came from.

Dad had old-fashioned values and knew the importance of sticking to your path and not straying from it. He would always say to me, 'I don't mind what qualifications you have as long as you've got a PhD in common sense.' Dad was all about thinking things through. His philosophy was: don't make assumptions about people or stereotype or disregard them because of their background or their colour, culture or whatever. Give people the benefit of the doubt and treat them with respect and dignity. Dad never lost his strong Jamaican accent the whole time he lived in Britain.

When Dad's venture into property turned sour, our family was forced to move into a single room. But in 1968, Dad was able to buy a house in Hornsey. I had my own room and we had a phone – we'd arrived! In the kitchen, pride of place went to the gas stove. Every Sunday without fail, Dad would dismantle the stove, clean all its parts and then reassemble it. After he'd done that, he would line up everyone's shoes and polish them. During the week, if our shoes had started to lose their lustre, he would buff them up. My sister and I had the shiniest shoes in school. The stove and our shoes were Dad's Sunday ritual. Watching the methodical way he took the stove apart gave me an understanding and an appreciation of patience; of not being too quick to move on – or as Mum and Dad used to say, 'Don't act in haste and repent at leisure.'

The third part of Dad's Sunday ritual was playing records on his radiogram. Dad loved Blue Beat, as it was called before it evolved into ska and then into reggae. He loved jazz too. It was through him that I got my first taste of jazz, long before I took up the trumpet and joined the jazz band in secondary school. It was quite amazing how he would get immersed in the music, as a form of relaxation with us before another hard week at work.

Dad's methodical nature really came to the fore when he was choosing schools for us to go to. He wouldn't just settle for the one that was nearest to us; he took us round to see a few before choosing one. That was how I ended up going to Ashmount School in Hornsey Lane, rather than the primary school I'd originally wanted to attend, which was closer to home. Ashmount was an inspired choice. It was led by an amazing headmistress, Mrs Henshaw – a very dynamic woman. She treated her pupils well and was very supportive to us. Once, she gave me a book about Cleopatra to read. I read it and was very inspired, learning about this black woman who had been queen of Egypt.

Another teacher at Ashmount who was a big influence on me was Mr Williams, our Head of Music. He would always play Tchaikovsky or Beethoven or Mozart to calm us down after playtime. It's thanks to him that I developed an appreciation for classical music, which I have to this day, mainly through the virtuoso Andrea Bocelli.

Many of my schoolmates came from families that were very well off; their parents were all CEOs of banks or charities. One of them was the son of the actor Warren Mitchell, who was the star of the comedy show *Till Death Do Us Part*. It was always quite surreal seeing 'Alf Garnett' on TV at home, then going to school the next day and seeing him there picking up his son! Being around children from such wealthy backgrounds was a great learning experience for me. I learned from them the importance of networking and of having a group of close friends. I also became adept at 'code switching' – changing my vernacular to suit whatever environment I was in. I could speak like my rich schoolmates, think like them, and fit in when I went to their houses and their parties.

The few years we'd spent in Jamaica helped me develop a can-do attitude and to see that I could be anything I wanted to be. I saw black politicians, black police officers and black doctors in Jamaica. When I came back to England and returned to primary school, I could confidently say I wanted to be a doctor. Even when my teachers would say, 'Are you sure?', I could say yes with confidence because I had seen that it was possible for me to be one. My black classmates who were born in the UK but had never been to any other developing country just couldn't fathom it. I had a totally different mindset. Even later on, when I started thinking about going into policing, the concept of a black cop wasn't alien to me because I'd seen black policemen in Jamaica. Those formative years in Jamaica taught me not to have a stunted view of life, or to put a ceiling on what I was capable of, through a free mind unshackled by any form of mental slavery.

Every day after school I would go home, do my chores, wash up, and make sure Hyacinth was taken care of. Hyacinth was in my school's nursery section. I would take her home; we'd both get changed out of our uniforms and then do our chores. There was no idling around. Mum finished work at about half past four in the afternoon. When she came home, she would check that I had done everything I was meant to do. Hyacinth and I were latchkey kids, which was commonplace in those days. You weren't seen as vulnerable, or as a target for people. Where we lived, the general attitude was very much an 'open door' one. We knew all our neighbours, and all the neighbours looked out for us.

Dad was on the case again when it came to choosing a secondary school. In fact, we started visiting prospective secondary schools three years before I was due to leave primary school! Out of all the schools we visited, Highbury Grove Boys School seemed the most promising. It had a good reputation, and its facilities were second to none. The headmaster was Dr Rhodes Boyson, who later became Education Secretary under Margaret Thatcher. It was a massive school; over a thousand boys went there.

After visiting Highbury Grove, I told Mrs Henshaw that I was considering applying to go there. She said, 'It's a grammar school, so if you do want to go there, you'll have to take the 11-plus exam.' I was determined to do whatever it took to get in, but then the school changed and became a comprehensive, and so I didn't have to take the 11-plus. I went for an interview and Dr Boyson was on the panel. He didn't say anything; he just sat, monitored my interview for a while, then moved on to the next panel and did the same thing. I think he was just making sure he had an idea of who was coming to his school.

Once my place at Highbury Grove was secured, Dad plotted a route for getting me safely to school and back every day: 'Go up Hornsey Road and get the 210 bus to Finsbury Park. That way you miss the record shop in Seven Sisters Road' which was where the cops regularly swooped under the 'Sus Law'. The record shop he was referring to was a specialist shop that sold reggae records. It was a focal point for people, especially on a Friday afternoon when they had just got paid. A lot of black youngsters would go there, legitimately, to buy records. But then you'd get the odd person smoking drugs, and that would attract the local cops. The shop that sold soul records in the area didn't attract the same sort of police attention. Looking back, that's probably one reason I wasn't into reggae all that much, avoiding the reggae shop so as to steer clear of the police who focused all their attention on it. Dad gave me a clear understanding of how you navigate through the raindrops; how you avoid the snares and traps. Long before 'risk assessment' became a buzz phrase, my dad was running risk assessments on everything. He would always say, 'Check things out, look at things closely before you act.'

There was a lot going on at Highbury Grove to distract an eleven-year-old. As with any boys' school, there was much jockeying for position; it was one unending contest to prove you were the best footballer or sprinter. Unfortunately for me, I didn't excel in either. I could run and I could play football, but I wasn't at the top of either game. However, I was quite good at cricket, so I started to play that a lot more. I was a wicket keeper until I grew too tall; wicket keepers tend to be smaller compact people. I used to bat as well, but I wasn't exceptional at bowling. Through sheer persistence, I earned a reputation for playing cricket. Sport became a means by which I developed networks at Highbury Grove. Dad, meanwhile, was pleased that I had something to keep my mind active – especially during the long summer holidays. I also would look forward to batting practice with Dad in Finsbury Park, where he bowled balls with varied spin and pace to maintain my skills. This was quality time that forged a precious relationship between us, which I felt compelled to replicate with my children. Legacy!

Peer pressure was very strong in those days, but nothing like it is now, especially with social media to contend with. In those days, parental pressure carried more weight than peer pressure. Mum was the expert at vetting my friends. She would take one look at them and say, 'Don't let that one come into my house' and that would be it. It might have felt harsh at the time, but looking back, I can see how it saved me from some awful situations. Just before we moved into the new house, we lived in a bedsit just up the road, and I used to run around the local building sites with some of the boys who lived nearby, scrumping for pears and berries. One day, one of them said, 'We're going up to the old train tracks to meet some girls – do you want to come?' I said, 'I haven't got permission to do that; my parents told me I can't go further than here.' Two days later, I heard that three of them were alleged to have committed a gang rape. I couldn't believe it. That was when I realized how peer pressure could get you into some life-changing situations. It stayed with me all through my years in secondary school. Whenever someone came along and said, 'Let's try this' or 'Let's try that', I would hear Dad say, 'Just think what could happen.' Sometimes I would say to my dad, 'Why are you giving me such a hard time?' and he would reply, 'Who else is going to give you a hard time? That's my job!' Thanks to the practical advice I got from both Mum and Dad, I got through Highbury Grove relatively unscathed.

I started to play the trumpet in my first year of secondary school. Tony Cookson was our trumpet teacher; I was walking along the corridor where the music rooms were one day, and overheard him playing in one of the practice rooms. He played so well, I was immediately hooked. Tony didn't just teach us how to play the trumpet. More than that, he taught us how to be men: how to conduct yourself, even how to sit, your breath, your poise, your mannerisms. I suppose I could have got all that from another teacher, but there was just something special in the way Tony conveyed it to us. I still meet up with one of my old school friends who also learned the trumpet, Junior Douglas, and we still talk about Tony Cookson, including the legacy he left behind after his death

After the near-death experience I'd had back in Jamaica, I've always felt protected. Not invincible or untouchable; I've just always felt that if I stuck to my path, I would be protected. Mum had a set of Bible verses she would always repeat to me; one of them was Numbers 23:20 – 'I have received a command to bless; he has blessed, and I cannot change it.' No man can curse whom God has blessed. Mum believed that with all her heart and ensured I did so too.

Highbury Grove gave me many avenues for growth. I wasn't a model student, but I knew the choices I made could be life-changing, so I did my best to make the right ones. Dad was always on hand to remind me, 'You've got to use common sense in the choices you make.' Not everyone in the school had their dads living with them, but I always came to Parents' Evening with both my parents. They never missed one, even when the feedback they received from my teachers about me wasn't great.

In January 1973, a new boy, who was destined to become a life-long friend, joined Highbury Grove. Leslie McGregor John was born in London but grew up in New York, where he'd soaked up all the music and culture that he could. Today, he's better known as Leee John, leader of the band Imagination, with whom he had a string of chart hits in the 1980s. When Leee joined Highbury Grove, he brought an explosion of culture with him. He had a massive cassette player, known as a ghetto blaster, that he always carried around; invariably you would hear him before you saw him. He spoke with an American accent and was very much into black empowerment. Leee had our music teacher Terry Stockwell eating out of his hand. I was very close to Tony Cookson, the trumpet teacher, so I didn't really know Terry – even though he ran the jazz band and I'd joined it. At this point, I'd turned my back a bit on my other subjects, which I shouldn't have, in hindsight. But for a while, I really thought I was going to be a full-time musician, and this was when the jazz band started. We played all over the country – in Birmingham, Bristol and several other towns and cities. We even went to Germany. We played old-style jazz: Glenn Miller, Dizzy Gillespie, that sort of thing. When Leee arrived, he became our lead singer. He was a major influence on us, with his stories about his experiences living in New York.

My education in black culture had started a year or two before Leee joined our school, at the Black House – a cultural centre and bookshop on Holloway Road. The Black House was originally started by Michael de Freitas, a Trinidadian-born civil rights activist who changed his name to Michael X. He had quite a chequered life and was convicted of murder and executed in Trinidad in 1975. We would go to the Black House during our lunch breaks and after school, and spend hours reading up on black history and about Africa. I had a lot of friends from various African countries; they'd tell me what life in their countries was like. I could see the parallels with the years I'd spent in Jamaica; how I'd been able to see black people in positions there that I didn't in England. My Nigerian friends and I would talk about stuff that lifted our eyes from our current experience to where we wanted to be. We had a great soundtrack to accompany our conversations – from James Brown exhorting us to 'Say It Loud, I'm Black and I'm Proud' to Bob and Marcia reminding us that we were 'Young, Gifted and Black'.

In the autumn of 1973, I went to Hackney College. I had to retake a couple of O Levels because although I was at the top of my game music-wise, I'd let other subjects slip. I retook the O Levels and did A Level physics, chemistry and biology. Hackney College was quiet, and I found I could focus on my work better. However, the area itself used to attract some horrible people. On one occasion I was leaving the building one evening when some guy just smashed a glass. 'Gosh, man,' I said. 'Children come here to play; they could get injured!'

Who told me to say that? The guy chased me with a knife! Fortunately, I was able to outrun him, but I needed to pause for breath, so I took refuge in a nearby chip shop. I ran in and jumped over the counter. The owner of the chip shop was in the middle of shouting 'Get out of my shop!' when the guy ran in and jumped on the counter, knife in hand.

In my mind's eye, I could see the six-year-old me being tossed about helplessly in the Rio Grande. Was this it? Saved from drowning in Jamaica, just to be killed by some random guy in Hackney because I wanted children to play safely? It all seemed so pointless. Fortunately for me, the chip shop owner wasn't having it. He yelled, 'Get off my counter!' then he picked up the cleaver he used to chop fish and said, 'Get out now, or I'll chop your foot off!' The guy jumped off the counter and legged it.

Crisis over, the chip shop owner ordered me to leave. I said, 'Listen, please – just give me a few minutes to make sure he's really gone.' I tore out of that chippy and did not stop running for about a mile. I didn't bother waiting for a bus; I kept running through back streets over Green Lanes through to Finsbury Park. I'd never run so fast for so long in my life before.

But again, I just felt relieved and blessed that I had got through that situation. And then it struck me that I might bump into him again when I went to college the next day, even though he wasn't a student there. And I did – but he saw me, and it was as if nothing had happened.

I had some other encounters that made me think Mum's prayers were working. Once when I was in primary school, I stepped out onto the road from behind a parked ice cream van. I wasn't looking and a car came up screeching, stopping just inches away from me. I could have been killed on the spot. I never told my parents about that one; they would have told me to keep out of danger!

Omar Atie was one of my schoolmates who'd chosen to go to Kingsway College when I opted for Hackney College. One day in December 1976, he invited me to a Christmas disco they were having. 'I've got a blind date for you,' he said. The blind date's name was Gretl Kraus. She was half Nigerian and half Austrian, and had recently come over from Nigeria to study in the UK.

Omar hadn't gone into any detail about Gretl, beyond 'There's this girl I'd like you to meet'. When I arrived at the venue, I had no idea who I was supposed to be meeting. I scanned the room but didn't see any girls who looked like they were waiting for a blind date to show up. As it turned out, she'd been involved in a traffic accident on her way to the disco. Fortunately, the accident wasn't serious. When she did eventually arrive, she was remarkably composed, given what she'd just been through.

It wasn't love at first sight when Gretl and I met. In fact, my first impressions were that she was a bit too tomboyish for me. She was dressed very casually in a checked red lumberjack shirt and jeans. Then again, I wasn't expecting the event to be too dressy, given that we were all students. She had a strong Nigerian accent. Most of my friends back then were Nigerian, so it was nothing I wasn't already used to. She looked very young for 17, but when she spoke, she came across as very mature and composed.

We didn't say much to each other during that first date. We danced more than we talked. When we danced, I noticed that she liked to lead. I did wonder if that was an indication of how any possible relationship we had would go!

We decided to meet again after Christmas, and then had a few more follow-up dates, usually around Lancaster Gate where she lived. I would meet her at the beauty school where she was studying in Knightsbridge, and we would go to the Stockpot restaurant off Sloane Street. As we got to know each other more, I found her to be really down to earth and very easy-going. She wasn't at all like a lot of the young women I knew. I found her way of looking at things very interesting. She wasn't impressed by material things. Nothing mesmerized her.

I thought things were going well between us, but suddenly she lost touch, around the time that her elder sister, Betty, gave birth to her first child. I thought, 'Oh well, it was nice while it lasted,' and assumed it was over. Then one day, Leee and I were walking along Tottenham Court Road window-shopping when someone jumped on my back. For a split second, I thought someone was trying to mug me – then I turned around and saw that it was Gretl.

'What are you doing?' I said. 'You could have got hurt!'

'Betty saw you,' she replied, pointing to where her sister was standing across the road. 'She told me to call you over.'

'And how come I never heard from you these past few weeks?' I asked.

Gretl explained that her mum had come over from Nigeria for the delivery of Betty's baby, and she'd been worried that her mum wouldn't approve of her having a Jamaican boyfriend, even though Betty had tried to reassure her that things would be fine. There was only one way to find out, so we arranged for me to come around to their place and meet their mum. Gretl needn't have worried; as soon as I walked in, her mum went, 'I like this one!'

It was a gradual process, but I knew from very early on that Gretl was to feature very prominently in my life and become my wife. When I shared these thoughts with Gretl's cousin, Kunle Ogundipe, at one of his prestigious Kensington house parties, he almost laughed his socks off, believing I didn't stand a chance of doing so. I started to have my doubts when she went back to Nigeria after finishing her studies in 1978, but to my amazement we remained pen pals for the few years we were apart, except for my visits to Lagos for Christmas and Gretl's summer visits.

2

'Do I look like a white racist?'

My time at Hackney College whetted my appetite for science. After doing my A-levels, I got a place on the Applied Biology degree course at North East London Polytechnic, now known as UEL (University of East London). Dad was really pleased that I was doing science. I graduated in 1980 and started working at the Royal Free Hospital in Hampstead soon after. My ultimate aim was to become a doctor or work in the pharmaceutical industry, and I had the route planned out: I would work as a research scientist for a few years, then make the transition over to medicine.

One late spring morning when I was dashing along Water Lane from the Romford Road building to the Maryland site, I was stopped in my tracks by the sight of a black uniformed police officer in a marked police vehicle, talking on his radio in a strong authoritative voice. His shirt looked extra white on his dark Nubian skin. I paused, momentarily thinking 'You are a brave guy but what a role model.' Little did I know this non-verbal encounter would be a factor in my career path.

Having landed a job in one of the most progressive medical schools of the day, I felt the plan was off to a flying start. In the 1980s, the Royal Free was the most modern teaching hospital in London. Its medical unit was world renowned for its work in the field of gastroenterology, particularly on liver disease. So great was its reputation, we once had the Egyptian President Hosni Mubarak as a patient. When you have heads of state coming to a unit for treatment, you know its reputation is solid. Dame Sheila Sherlock was head of the unit, an internationally acclaimed liver specialist.

We were doing clinical trials of drugs and developing an invasive test around the impact of chemotherapy on patients, especially children. I had my own lab and was working with a small team. Roy Pounder, my boss, was the main medical consultant for the pharmaceutical company Smith Kline & French, as it was called then (it's now GlaxoSmithKline). We did invasive clinical trials for a lot of their drugs and for some other anti-cancer agents to see how those drugs impacted the lower bowel.

At times, the job could be heartbreaking, especially when children were involved. Cancer therapy in the early 1980s was quite crude in comparison to how it is today, and seeing a child suffer was nerve-wracking. Sadly, we sometimes lost them, which was always very painful.

When I wasn't working, I used to do a lot of sport, mainly squash. The Royal Free had great sports facilities with squash courts, a swimming pool, a gym, a basketball court and indoor football pitches. It was like some of these new so-called 'exclusive' gyms; it just happened to be in a hospital. I loved it. I could synchronize my analysis tests, go for a run, come back and read the results, and then play squash. The gym was also great for socializing. I used to meet all sorts of people there, and spend time chitchatting with them.

I was still in my international romance with Gretl, and the job gave me the flexibility to travel to Nigeria to see her, or time to be with her whenever she came over to the UK. I was getting an income, so I was able to do quite a lot more. I was a lot more independent. I really was in my comfort zone.

In late 1982, I was coming up to my third year in the job. I was twenty-five and thinking of moving into the sales side of the pharmaceutical industry. I have a very outward-looking personality, and I felt that I could use that more in the sales side of the industry, rather than being stuck in a lab all day. So I started applying for jobs. But every job I went for, I was being knocked back; I wasn't even getting interviews. I was either overqualified or under-experienced. I couldn't get my head around that; how could you be both? When the time came for my annual appraisal, I was very open with Roy about the fact that I wanted a career change.

Roy said, 'Leroy, I like your work, your energy and your ability, but I don't see you being in a lab – or in the pharmaceutical industry – for the next thirty-odd years.'

'What you think I should do then?' I asked.

'You know what?' he replied. 'I think your personality suits you being a cop.'

I looked at him and my perceptions came to mind: 'Do I look like a white racist?'

'You like to talk to people,' Roy continued, unaware of what he'd sparked off in my head.

Having grown up in the 1960s and 1970s, my love for cops was far from great. As already mentioned, these were the times of the Suspected Person law, or the Sus law, as it was more commonly known. The police in Britain had been using 'Stop and search' as far back as the nineteenth century, when the Vagrancy Act of 1824 was introduced to clamp down on begging and rough sleepers. The Sus law was a direct descendant of Section 4 of the Vagrancy Act. Under it, a police officer only needed to have suspicions about someone for them to stop that person or make an arrest. The sad reality was that, for far too many cops in Britain in the 1970s, all you needed to do to arouse their suspicions was have black skin. Consequently, we called them the Thought Police. They were responsible for stigmatizing and/or criminalizing legions of black people, before the law was repealed in the early 1980s, forming a stain of racial profiling that is still prominent in the black community's perception of policing.

Even as a schoolboy, I suffered as a result of the Sus law. Dad's meticulously planned route home from Highbury Grove may have spared me from running into cops on Seven Sisters Road or at the reggae record shop in Finsbury Park, but he hadn't reckoned with them showing up outside the school building itself. More than once, I was stopped by the police – in front of my school, in my school uniform and with my trumpet case in my hand. On several occasions, I would be going home after music practice, and cops would stop me. My dad saw this happen once at the school entrance after band practice as I was waiting for him to pick me up and he got really upset with the officers. By this time, Dad was working as a long-distance driver and he was always getting stopped, so he didn't have much love for cops either. He didn't like the way they talked to him. He was always very respectful when talking to people, and he felt that cops were very heavy-handed and disrespectful, and they didn't give people the dignity they deserved – which they really ought to have, given that they were public servants.

I told Roy that I would think about what he'd said. I was due to catch up with Gretl later that day, and I was quietly confident that she would tell me not to even think about it. But to my total amazement, when I told her about Roy's suggestion at the appraisal, she didn't dismiss it. Instead she said, 'I really think that's something you should consider.' About the same time, I began recalling the non-verbal encounter I had with the black officer I saw during my degree study days, and the vision of him sitting in his police car grew in rapidity and intensity in my mind.

Quite a few people who didn't work at the Royal Free used the hospital's sports facilities. There were two guys in particular I had come to know who used the gym very frequently. I would also see them in the pool, and we would occasionally chat in the bar. After bumping into them a few times, I found out that they were off-duty cops.

Meeting these two guys helped me see the human side of police officers. They talked about regular things like everyone else; they even offered to take me on some 'drive-arounds' in the back of their car. The drive-arounds were fun. The guys were really nice and easy-going, although part of me did think, 'This is Hampstead; police officers here won't be dealing with the sort of aggravation they would have somewhere like Hackney.' I started to feel that this was some kind of calling that I had to follow through. I did more research, and in September 1982, I submitted an application to join the Metropolitan Police.

I couldn't believe it when I had an interview a few weeks after applying. And then within a few days of doing the interview, I was offered a position. It all seemed to be happening a bit too quickly, so I asked for my appointment to be delayed, to buy myself some time to think about it a bit more. They agreed. My start date was deferred to June 1983.

In the meantime, I continued working at the Royal Free. I was at work there one autumn day that year when I received a phone call from my mum saying that my dad had been beaten up by some cops.

Dad had been out on a job, and he had decided to get some lunch. He'd parked his van up near the local fish and chip shop and went in. These two police officers called him out of the chippy and said, 'You're causing an obstruction with your vehicle.' He said, 'Well, I've done it so many times here and it's never been an obstruction.' The officers got tetchy with him, and he said to them, 'If you're going to book me, then just book me.'

Dad was a very meticulous man; if he was going to end up in court over the way his vehicle was parked, then he was definitely going to make sure that the evidence for his defence was all in order. He prided himself on that. So he started to measure the distance between the offside of his vehicle and the other vehicle on the other side of the road. He was in the middle of doing this when the two officers laid into him. They beat him senseless, then took him to the police station and charged him with resisting arrest. After being charged and bailed at Holloway Police Station for unnecessary obstruction and resisting arrest, he made his way to the hospital.

I rushed straight from the Royal Free to Whittington Hospital in Islington. The cops had beaten Dad so badly, I actually walked past him in the A&E department and didn't recognize him. I've never sensed as much hate as I did when I saw Dad leaning backwards, with swollen black and blue eyes. I could smell it; I could taste it. If a police officer had walked into the room at that very moment, I would have launched myself at him. I really had to control the rage that I felt that day, otherwise it would have consumed me. Thankfully, I've never had that feeling again ever since.

***

'Forget it,' I said to Gretl. 'I'm not going to be a cop after what they did to Dad.'

'Maybe that's the reason you should join,' Gretl said.

'Don't be silly,' I replied. 'What can I do about a whole police service?'

But Gretl persisted – and when I spoke to Roy about it at work the next day, he said the same thing. A few days later, I met the guys in the bar, and I was a bit abrupt, even though I eventually shared Dad's arrest with them. Their response was: 'Don't judge a whole organization by a few bad officers.' In the end, I decided not to withdraw my application, as I'd already delayed it till June.

In early 1983, I got my own apartment in Islington. It was situated right next to the Arsenal Stadium, the ideal location for someone who has been a 'Gooner' since the age of eleven! I loved the flat, and I immediately began to warm to the idea of policing the area. I still hadn't told my parents that I was considering joining the police, especially after what had happened to my dad. How could I tell him that I was going to join the same organization that the people who had beaten him senseless were part of?

I still felt the need to seek counsel from someone older, so I spoke to Leee's mum, Jessie Stephens. She was on the local Police Community Advisory Group, a real advocate for building bridges between the police and the public. 'I really sensed that I need to give this a try,' I said to her. 'We need an organization that looks like London,' she replied. 'We need black officers.' That conversation with Leee's mum was the clincher for me, especially as I still hadn't told my dad yet.

When I applied to join the police, I put my parents' address on the application. I informed Scotland Yard of my new address when I moved. Back then, if you were about to join the police, they would send an officer to your address to assess the area and to ensure a person would not be exposed to unnecessary risk on joining the police. I knew where we were living was no problem. Then one day, I received a concerned phone call from Dad, saying that there were police officers at his door.

'Why?' I asked. 'Does it have anything to do with that assault on you?'

'No,' Dad replied. 'It's you they're after.'

'What do you mean?'

'Do I look like a white racist?'

'They're telling me you're going to become a cop.'
'Oh Dad, I've been wanting to tell you…' but he'd hung up before I could finish the sentence.

3

Training days

I knew I had to put my case to Dad at the very least, and hope that he would understand. Still feeling crushed from the abrupt phone conversation, I rushed over to my parents' house.

'Listen, Dad,' I said when we finally caught up, 'I've thought about this a lot, and I really want to try it. If my character starts to change and I become some hard-nosed right-winger, I'll leave in a heartbeat.'

By this time, I had started to formulate a vision of being a policeman, the calling I believed I had and all that entailed. I poured out my heart to Dad and told him all that I had envisioned. He didn't say much; he was still very upset – not simply because of his personal feelings about the police, but more because I had decided to turn my back on medicine and science. Going from being a scientist to being a cop was, to him, a retrograde step. I guess his negative experience with cops reinforced that for him. Either way, I needed Dad on my side – not just with the job, or my wedding, coming up, but for his love.

***

I woke up on the morning of 21 May 1983 feeling as though I hadn't had any sleep the night before – which was odd, given that as far as stag nights go, mine had been a bit of a non-event.

Leee was my best man and the stag night he organized was a bunch of us guys sitting round drinking at his house. I'd left them to it after a while and gone to bed early. Leee had a car booked to take me to Finsbury Town Hall in Rosebery Avenue for the first part of the wedding. But the car turned up late. Not a good start to the day…

The route most people used for driving from Hendon to Islington involved going via Swiss Cottage. I could sense that the traffic round that way would be heavy, so I said to the driver, 'Do not go via Swiss Cottage' – which he promptly ignored, and we got stuck in Saturday shoppers' traffic. I was agitated and felt helpless. This was long before mobile phones, so I had no way of letting Gretl know what was going on. Gretl, meanwhile, had already arrived. Her car was going around and round Finsbury Town Hall to kill time as she waited for her groom to turn up. 'You'll be late for your own funeral!' Dad said when we eventually arrived, to which I replied, 'That's not such a bad idea!'

I had a bit of a rant at Leee and anyone else I considered responsible, but cooled down when Gretl turned up looking resplendent and regal. I hadn't seen much of her lately; she had gone to Nigeria to spend time with her mum who was unable to come to London for the wedding. Her dress was beautiful, and she looked absolutely radiant, with the Princess Diana hairstyle that was all the rage at the time.

As soon as the registry office ceremony ended, we made our way to Gospel Oak Methodist Church in Belsize Park for the blessing. We didn't use the traditional vows; instead we adapted our own, dedicating ourselves to each other. The reception took place in a function room in the Royal Free around the corner. From the beginning and end of the day, so many people seemed to be fussing around Leee instead of me and Gee; you would have thought he was the one getting married! As Imagination's lead singer, it was to be expected, for a member of one of the most prominent London soul bands at the time. At least his best

27

man speech did me proud and he has walked the talk ever since as my best mate.

***

I had barely been married a month when it was time to start my police training.

To Dad's credit, he drove me to Hendon Police College the night before the start of my training period. I'll always respect him for putting his own misgivings aside to support me. That kind gesture bonded us together in a very special way. It was 19 June, a hot sultry Sunday, and I was to start the following morning.

Leaving the quiet, sterile environment of science research for the macho, militaristic culture of Hendon was a massive culture shock. You could smell the testosterone in the air the moment you passed through the gates into the campus. That first night was a restless one for me. My room was very basic; a small student unit with just a bed, a sink and a wardrobe. I sat on the bed, surveyed the spartan surroundings and tried to prepare myself spiritually for all I was about to face over the following 20 weeks. I knew it was going to be tough; I was also very much aware that I would be a minority. Even back in those days, the NHS had nurses, doctors and scientists from different backgrounds and from all over the world. I just knew the police would be different, and that I would be one of very few black people there.

That evening, I took a walk around the campus and ended up in the canteen. Everyone was in regular clothing, so at first glance it looked just like any normal canteen you'd find anywhere else. But then I started to overhear bits of the conversations the other guys were having. Immediately I got a sense of what I was up against. Some of them were quite strong in their views about the world, and saw things in a very 'them and us' way, with the police being the 'us' and the rest of the public as 'them'. I found that quite disappointing, as I've always felt that the public and the police should be together. We are public servants after all. Sadly, that 'them and us' mindset I picked up on in the canteen on my first night at Hendon never changed throughout my 30 years in the Met.

I didn't sleep a wink that night. I woke up extra early, got myself ready and bumped into Tom Kelly, the guy who would become our class captain. We had adjoining rooms. It was great having such a role model as Tom around. Prior to joining the police, he had been a drill instructor and a trainer of senior officers at Sandhurst. He was very organized and knew not only how to look the part, but also how to think the part. Going from the military to the police is quite a smooth transition – definitely much more so than going from medical research to the police!

Tom taught me how to buff up my shoes to an eye-piercing shine and to get the best creases when I ironed my uniform. Most importantly, he taught me how to change my learning style so that I could recite key points verbatim; parrot fashion. A key element of what we had to learn were legal definitions and procedural text known as 'A reports'. Our teaching on any given subject would be focused on bold type A reports for that subject matter, and there was a good chance these would come up in exams. You still needed to know the other texts, of course, but the items in bold were things you needed to know word for word.

For me, learning to memorize A reports was quite difficult because it was a totally different way of processing information than I was accustomed to. As a research scientist, you had to know your subject in such a way that you were able to discuss it, not just regurgitate it. You need to have a rationale for your discussions. With A reports, you didn't even need to understand them fully; you either memorized them properly or you didn't. Tom had been doing this sort of learning from the get-go. He and I sat together in the canteen that morning for our first Hendon breakfast. It was a very basic, buffet-style affair: eggs and beans, both overcooked. I took one look at it and thought, 'I am not going to put on any weight in this place!' In fact, I lost weight during my training period because I hardly ate. I couldn't wait to get home at the weekend to eat some proper food.

I went and got my timetable and met my other classmates. There were about 20 of us in the class, and we did everything together. Our drills involved marching from one end of the estate to the other. None of us knew how to do the drills, but Tom – not just ex-military, but a former drill instructor – got us whipped into shape quicker than the others. He was brilliant. He made the training fun, and we got into the swing of it very quickly. I felt very fortunate that I had someone like him, of a similar age group, a few years older than the teenage majority, to help with the transition from lab culture to police culture. It helped me to put aside certain assumptions and see the importance of keeping my head down and getting on with what I needed to get on with. It was easier said than done, but my attitude was 'You're in it now, just get on with it.'

We would line up along Peel Road for the morning inspections, and the Intake Manager would call people out if their shoes or their uniforms or anything else were not up to scratch. Anyone who didn't meet the mark cast a shadow over the rest of the class, ending up in some form of class detention. It really was like being back in school.

In class, the instructor asked each one of us why we had decided to join the police. I told him that I wanted to be a public servant, and that I thought it was important that the Met looked like the community it served. I said that I was a team player, but I wasn't there to make friends; I was there to work effectively. 'I'm not here to ingratiate myself with anyone,' I said. 'I'm here to do the best I can and be judged on my merits.'

Looking back, I think I may have put it across a bit too bluntly. But I felt it was important for me to spell out what I stood for. At 26, I was at least eight years older than most of my classmates. Other than Tom, myself and a couple of others, the average age of our crop of recruits was about 20. I was married and Gretl was pregnant with our first child. I'd had a profession before – and my ex-boss had left me an open door to return to it, if I decided policing wasn't for me after all – so I wasn't relying solely on this as a permanent job. I thought I needed to set my stall out that I was a black man who happened to be a cop and not a cop who happened to be black. I was determined not to be like the policemen I'd had bad encounters with as a youngster, or the ones who'd assaulted my dad, but like the role model black officer in the panda car I observed in the 1970s.

It was disheartening having lunch in the canteen and hearing fellow recruits casually peppering their conversations with the P-word and the N-word. I'm not the sort of person who puts up with that, but obviously you can't take on every single battle or you'll be fighting all the time. I had to be wise and step clearly and decisively when necessary, especially being so young in service.

One thing I was very fortunate about was having my old school friend Leee John nearby. As Leee's band Imagination had been so successful, he'd bought a house about five-minutes walk from Hendon. Leee's semi-detached house became my oasis during my training period. I very rarely bothered going to the pub with the other recruits after a day at training school; instead, I would pop round to Leee's house, which was always full of artistic, creative people. Some of them I knew, some I didn't, but with my own musical background, I fitted in quite easily. It always felt like coming up for air, experiencing something totally opposite to what I'd been doing all day.

I sometimes found it difficult to go back to Hendon after an evening of great conversation, decent soul food and fine champagne at Leee's house. Part of me would question why one would leave a reasonably comfortable lifestyle for an insensitive culture that didn't celebrate diversity and was very narrow in its thinking. But I had to be disciplined and stick to what I'd started – even though I'd questioned my sanity from my first week at Hendon.

Policing seemed to attract people who are quite set in their ways, very narrow in how they perceive others, and who enjoy sticking very rigidly to the occupational cultural rules of always backing up your mates and defending the Met regardless; a form of blind loyalty. When it comes to crime, such people can be quite insensitive about what's behind it. As a result, you end up with an organization that's tough on crime but doesn't really think about the causes of it, and perpetuates the 'them' – the public – and 'us' mindset. It was clear to me even at these early stages that the average officer was generally right wing in thinking and seem to identify with Enoch Powell's 1968 'Rivers Of Blood' speech and its concerns over mass immigration from the Commonwealth.

***

I strongly believed that if it wasn't for the parents I had, I could easily have become a criminal suspect. Had it not been for the nurturing and love I received from them, I could have fallen foul of peer pressure and got into all sorts of difficulties. The memory of the boys from my old neighbourhood who had got involved in a gang rape never left me, ensuring that I held my values and beliefs close to my inner being. It also emphasized the importance of peer pressure, especially for young people surrounded by dysfunctional role models.

In contrast to the parrot-fashion style of learning necessary for the theory side of our operational work, I found the practicals much easier to get into. The training ground had mock roads, shops, a police station and post office; here we would act out various real-life scenarios. A basic scenario would involve a motorist failing to acknowledge someone at a pedestrian crossing, or one of the trainers pretending to be driving while drunk. We would stop the vehicle and repeat to the motorist the offence they'd just committed. In the drink-drive scenario, we would ask the motorist to take a breathalyser test, and then move on to the make-believe police station and present evidence to the station sergeant (as they were known then).

As well as traffic scenarios, we would also run through incidents such as robberies, assaults or thefts, with other officers acting as the suspects. Sometimes staff members would act too; if there were two staff members supervising us, one would play the villain in one of our scenarios while the other one observed us. If only policing in the real world were as simple as those scenarios sometimes made it seem!

My time at Hendon was a year before the 1984 Police and Criminal Evidence Act (PACE) came into force, so we were trained in accordance with the Metropolitan Police Act of 1866. Before PACE, if an officer stopped you in the street, they had no obligation to explain why they'd stopped you – and so most officers just didn't. Nowadays, an officer has to give a full explanation to anyone they stop as to why, and there's a code of practice that dictates how officers interact with members of the public. I always thought it was common courtesy to tell people why I was stopping them, who I was and where I was stationed, so that they would feel they were being treated with respect and dignity.

During the early weeks of my training, I was enlisted to be part of a recruiting campaign and was bussed out of Hendon to do some photoshoots. Some of my colleagues felt a bit resentful, and there were murmurs about me being given special treatment. Some of them actually confronted me and said this, to which I replied, 'There aren't many black people in this organization and they're trying to recruit more, so it's only sensible that they'd ask me to be involved in marketing initiatives like this. I wouldn't worry about it; if you were black, I'm sure they'd have picked you.'

They just stared at me blankly. I don't think they ever got my point of view. And I suppose that's still the case today. People do see me as a bit of a lone wolf or a maverick. Both within the Met and within the African-Caribbean community, I've encountered people who would accuse me of betraying my culture and not being sincere or loyal. But to me, loyalty means being ethical and to the point, and being truthful. I'm not into misplaced loyalties.

Everyone knew that Tom was going to be class captain, but it was a shock to all of us when I was appointed to be his deputy. The decision was not just based on ability to learn the theory and the practical, but also on sporting ability. Thanks to the training regime I'd initiated back at the Royal Free, I was very sporty and extremely fit. In between running lab tests, I regularly ran eight to ten miles, played squash or swam most days. I didn't have children then, so I could devote as much time to it as I liked. I even occasionally got Gretl to train with me – which she did until her pregnancy became too far advanced. At Hendon, being able to show your physical prowess was a sure way to get respect. Knowing your theory was fine; so too was knowing your practicals. But if you had physical presence, your chances of survival were much higher. There weren't that many people who could outrun me or do all the physical training – not even the boxing, which I had done a bit of as a Boy Scout during my schoolboy days.

Reluctantly and grudgingly, the others accepted me as deputy class captain – mainly because Tom said, in true military style: 'Leroy is my deputy. If I'm not around, you do what he tells you. If you don't, I'll fall on you like a ton of bricks.'

During my tenth week at Hendon, Gretl gave birth to our first son, Gerad, at the Royal Free Hospital. We named him after Gretl's father, whose name is actually Gerhard, but he once misspelled his name on a letter he wrote to us and we thought there was something charming about the name being spelled that way, so we stuck with it. I was still treated like staff at the Royal Free, and so Gretl had a private room (my old boss was still there when our other two children, Leah and Myles, were born; both times, he pulled some strings and got Gretl a private room, which was nice of him). The Royal Free is just down the road from Hendon, so I could visit that week. Our timetable had changed, so I had week 11 at home – which meant that when Gretl was discharged from the hospital, I was at home to support her during her first week back.

Gerad's birth was a welcome distraction from the culture at Hendon. Sometimes we'd be playing football, and you would hear someone mutter the N-word. I learned to respond to incidents like that without losing control. I wouldn't swear; I would just treat anyone who was nasty with the contempt that they deserved. The secret was not to let people know that you were sensitive about certain things. It was very insidious; it felt like a trap and I wasn't going to allow them to get through to me. You just had to develop a coping strategy suited to your strength of character and vulnerabilities.

I was able to pass on my coping strategy to another recruit from an Asian background. Dal Babu was born in Walsall, and had a teaching background and a few weeks less service than I had. He once shared with me his intention of resigning because he wasn't treated right. I said, 'Did you expect to be greeted with open arms?' I emphasized the need to earn respect and not to 'let the so and so's get you down'. Fortunately, it worked, and he completed his 30 years.

Having a wife and child gave me an even stronger resolve to push through and excel. It's amazing what you can do when you have to; when you've got to dig deep and get to that cutting edge. I find that I really operate better when I'm out of my comfort zone.

Before long, the 20 weeks were up, and it was time for our passing-out parade. It was a brilliant day, made all the more special for me by having both Gretl and Gerad there with my parents and my sister. The other trainees and I marched in the ranks in front of the then commissioner, Sir Kenneth Newman. Commissioner Newman was small in stature but big in spirit. He'd joined the Palestine Police in the 1940s, and then transferred to the Met when the Palestine Police was disbanded in 1948. He would never have been able to join the Met directly as there was a height restriction in place back then – which they had just got rid of when I joined. We paraded in front of him and took the salute.

There are times in life when opportunities come your way that enable you to be a part of something of huge significance; moments when everything around you just seems to be shouting out, 'This is your time – go for it!' Preachers often call such times 'kairos moments'. Those 20 weeks I spent at Hendon were that for me. They made it crystal clear to me that I had a calling for public service.

When I was assigned to Islington, I loved it because it was where I'd grown up. I knew the area and I loved the people. But as I was to find out, training school is no comparison to actually pounding the beat.

4

Police and thieves in the street

King's Cross Division included the police station at 227 Upper Street, right in the area where I grew up. I knew the area well and I felt comfortable working there. My biggest challenge was arresting people I'd gone to school with. I encountered people who had been through a lot of drug addictions, domestic violence problems, fights – you name it. I was very sympathetic. I realized how fortunate I was to have the parents I had, because I'd never felt unloved or exposed to the sort of risk some of the people I came across on the job had been through. I felt fortunate not to have been abused or exploited in any way.

Although I'd passed out from Hendon, I was still some way away from officially being a cop. I was only a third of the way through the two-year probationary period, and I would have to take an exam every month. But before all that, there was the question of which relief team I'd be assigned to.

When you joined a division in those days, you would spend ten weeks on the borough learning the ropes on a 'Street Duties' team. You did this before joining a response team: a 'relief' team, as they're known. At Islington, the most dreaded of the relief teams was A Relief.

Sergeant Alan Taplin ruled A Relief with an iron hand. He and the senior officers on the team seemed to delight in doing all they could to make probationers' lives absolute hell. Sergeant Taplin was Mr Miserable, the epitome of a drill sergeant major, even though he was never in the military. I think he was a frustrated military guy. At least he was consistent; he hated everyone! The other sergeants didn't appear to like themselves, let alone other people.

Sure enough, Sod's Law prevailed and I was assigned to A Relief. Getting the news was daunting; I'd heard all the horror stories of the many recruits who had fallen foul of the system. I decided to see it as a test. If I could get through the rest of my two years on A Relief, then I could definitely get through the other 28 years in the Met.

Sergeant Taplin did create a hostile environment on A Relief. You had to be able to speak up for yourself. In those days, probationers – commonly known as Sprogs – did all the donkey work and all the unsavoury jobs. If you were a probationer, you were literally his skivvy. He reflected that tough culture of the police at the time: don't show any empathy, be distant, be unapproachable. And as he was a senior sergeant, all the less experienced sergeants on A Relief followed suit.

The sergeants would allow the senior constables to do all sorts of things to wind us up. In the name of humour, they would take every opportunity to upset the sprogs, making comments such as 'If you can't take a joke you shouldn't have joined.' Sergeants were godlike figures to probationers like me. They could make or break a person's career, so I had to get on with them – even when I was convinced they didn't like me. Islington Division started from King's Cross and went all the way up to York Way and Caledonian Road. They'd give you the beat going right up Caledonian Road, and when you got there, call you back to make tea. All the probationers had to take turns to make the tea. If you were heard moaning about it, they would make you do it at the beginning and end of every day.

I decided I wasn't going to let them get to me. I'd make the tea when ordered to, but I'd make the worst weak and watery tea possible. When they complained, I'd say, 'I don't drink tea; I only drink coffee.' They knew I was playing up, and they disliked me for it. Fortunately, I could cope with this, because I was determined to be respected for my thief-taking and not for my tea-making.

I felt the streets were my sanctuary because, generally, the public was supportive. They gave words of encouragement, about me making a brave step in becoming a cop, but now and again I would get criticism from a small group of young people on Holloway Road, who would call me Judas. I would reply, 'How did you know that was my middle name?' It de-weaponized their verbal attacks and turned the verbal jousting into banter. The most vocal was Paul Anderson, in his late teens, who would offset his criticisms with questions, curious over why I had joined the Met. I willingly gave my reasons, followed by my musical anecdote that one of my favourite records, 'Police and Thieves', by Junior Murvin inspired me to become a cop and not a thief. I hoped our conversations meant something to him, but little did I know they were a precursor to us working together decades later in the new millennium.

You could say I was between a rock and a hard place, what with some negative community comments on one side, and on the other, the unprofessional and bigoted behaviour of my colleagues who were very suspicious of me. They couldn't get their heads round why this black guy – this black *graduate* – was joining the organization. They thought I was some sort of investigator or undercover reporter, and I used to play along. Whenever someone would ask what I was doing there, I would say, 'I'm writing a book.' I told them straight, 'I haven't come here to make friends. I've got loads of friends.'

That actually wasn't true any more. I'd lost many of my friends when I became a cop. If you want to cut your Christmas card list by 99 per cent, just join the police! However, in the process, I had come to realize that having a small handful of friends was enough. I wasn't looking at the job as a means of acquiring more mates. I will work with people and I'll work as part of a team, but I was determined to keep my professional life separate from my personal one. I observed how my fellow trainee officers treated one another in such a hard, insensitive way, and I wasn't surprised when they treated the public in the same way.

Becoming a new dad while at training school gave me a strength. On the job, it served as a reminder to my colleagues that I wasn't a youngster. At Hendon, even though I wasn't much older, the fact that I had a wife and child made me seem like a grandfather figure in my classmates' eyes. When I got to Islington, being an older guy imbued me with a bit more respect from the senior officers. They appreciated the fact that I wasn't naïve and unused to the world, especially the world of work.

I had one of the best arrest rates based on irrefutable evidence. I knew people were up to certain things; I heard of officers being economical with the facts and people complaining that certain officers had stitched them up – and I'd keep well away from those officers. If a certain group of cops accepted you, they would say to you, 'Jump in the car with us and we'll drive you around.' I wasn't interested. I liked walking; I still do. And so I'd walk along the back streets. One good consequence of that was that I had a great arrest rate. It made sense, really; you're not going to catch guys stealing cars or breaking into buildings if you're only walking on the main streets or driving around with blue lights and ear-piercing sirens, broadcasting your arrival.

I was the only one in our crop of probationers who'd come from Hendon. All the others were from another training establishment in Wanstead, and so they knew each other but none of them knew me. Again, the 'them and us' vibe reared its ugly head – only this time, the 'them' was me, the sole Hendon probationer, and the 'us' was all the Wanstead crew. I had an uphill task proving myself to them. Being local helped, because in briefings I was able to give them a lot of information about our beat. I'd say, 'I know that area; I used to play around there', or 'I went to school around there', or 'I shop around there.' Grudgingly, they accepted me.

One day, we had a call to a furniture shop on Essex Road, near the junction with New North Road. It was the end of a terrace of a parade of shops, and it had a flat roof that joined all of the shop fronts and doubled as a front porch for the two or three storeys of buildings behind it. One of the shops on this terrace was a furniture shop; someone had seen a burglar entering a house via the flat roof above it.

We surrounded the building, but there was no sign of the suspect. There weren't any sergeants present, but one of the senior constables said, 'Where's the sprog?'

Every eye turned towards the only probationer present: me.

'Shimmy up that pipe,' the senior constable said.

I took my coat off and shimmied up the pipe. As I was going over the wall that led onto the flat roof, I saw a pair of legs emerging out of a window. Connected to the legs was a torso, and on the back of this torso was a sack. The upper body and head emerged and turned nervously in my direction. 'Who are you?' he said.

'You're under arrest on suspicion of burglary,' I replied.

My colleagues down below called out, 'You alright, Leroy?'

'Yes,' I shouted back. 'I've got one here.'

As I was saying that, the burglar legged it. Above the shop fronts he went, with me in pursuit. I could see that the sack was weighing him down, banging against his back. Whatever its contents were, they were definitely very large. The chase was like a cartoon; he just needed the word SWAG written on his sack for it to have the full comic effect!

Eventually I caught up with him. There were no walls between each of the buildings and he was nearing the end of the terrace. I thought I'd better grab him, even if it was just to save him from himself. I'm not sure he knew he was nearing the end. All of a sudden, the solid flat rooftop transitioned into a very flimsy corrugated iron-type surface. I could see it; I don't know if he did because he was just running and looking to see if I was catching up with him – which wasn't difficult, because he had this heavy bag hitting him repeatedly in the back. I was wary that he might turn around and whack me with it. I grabbed him with the bag (hoping there weren't any sharp objects in it, or that he wasn't armed) – and as I did so, we both collapsed through the corrugated iron roof.

It was only an 18-foot drop, but it was the slowest 18 feet I've ever fallen in my life. The fall reminded me of when I did my swimming test for the Met. You jump off the high board and you think, 'When am I going to hit the water?'

I could see myself floating towards the floor. The burglar and I were in mid-air. He'd dropped the sack. It's amazing how time slows down (or seems to) when something like this happens. I could see we were in a workshop with lots of heavy machinery that we were about to land on, and I thought, 'That's going to hurt.' It was like a scene in the Leonardo DiCaprio film *Inception*; it all happened in seconds, but I still had time for an internal debate: 'How do I avoid hitting those machines?' There was a large metallic object right where I was about to land, and it would have done me a lot of damage.

We crash-landed on this huge chunk of metal. The burglar hit it and, in the process, pushed me slightly out of its path, but I did receive a glancing blow from it, which jarred my lower back. I heard the would-be burglar exhale in anguish, and I waited for whatever pain I'd incurred to kick in. It was the adrenalin that kicked in first.

I picked myself up and grabbed the semi-conscious burglar. 'I think it's best we call a doctor for you, mate,' I said. 'But why did you run in the first place?' He replied that he thought I was going to mug him for his stuff – even though I'd told him I was a police officer!

We called an ambulance, but he jumped up and said, 'I'm fine.' We took him to the station. In those days, as long as a suspect showed signs of being *compos mentis*, they were fine. Nowadays, you have to be extremely thorough. Back then, the thinking was that if you were a burglar, then being bumped about all over the place was an occupational hazard.

While we were booking him in, I felt a terrible pain in my back. I'd never had a pain like that in my life before then, and I'd done all sorts of sports. In the end, I had to be examined by a doctor, but it was a good 20 years later before the problem (a prolapsed disc) was diagnosed correctly.

In 30 years of police service, you do pick up injuries along the way. That back injury was the most significant one for me. The arrest itself was a boost to my career, especially in those early days. It opened up a network of burglars that we were able to infiltrate, and we acquired a lot of intelligence. That helped me to have a strong portfolio when I applied to join the CID later – even though it ultimately didn't help.

It didn't help much within the A Relief team either. It wasn't appreciated that I'd climbed up a pipe, arrested a burglar, injured myself but hadn't lost the prisoner – or that I'd identified all these other burglaries in the process. The response from my senior colleagues on A Relief was, effectively, that it was no big deal.

I used to love patrolling on my own on night duty. I was patrolling down Roman Way one night, just behind Pentonville Prison, when I noticed someone crouching down. I took my helmet off. He looked my way, but he just saw a dark-skinned guy in dark clothing. It was only when I walked straight up to him that he realized I was a police officer. His mate came from around the corner and I thought, 'Oh, I'm going to be in for a fight here.' I remember holding my truncheon, ready for trouble, but they both just submitted.

I informed them both that I was placing them under arrest for the attempted theft of hubcaps from a vehicle. I figured that there must be a vehicle somewhere around the corner the second guy had emerged from, so I radioed in for assistance.

When the other officers joined me, we had a look around the corner and found a van. Inside, it was like an Aladdin's cave of car parts, hubcaps and bumpers. You'd think I would have earned a few Brownie points for this discovery, but instead my name was mud at the station. I wasn't expecting hugs or a standing ovation, but at the same time I wasn't expecting the dirty look Sergeant Hayne gave me for bringing in the exhibits. If looks could kill, I would be six feet under.

I'd recovered so much stolen property, another sergeant had to help him book it all in. Needless to say, that sergeant wasn't too happy with me either. But I didn't care. As far as I was concerned, I had done my job. We had a lot of clear-ups of unsolved cases from that arrest. Several local people had reported having parts stolen from their cars; from their reports, we were able to identify those stolen parts in the stash that we'd recovered and restored some of them to their owners.

Every month, we would have to go to the divisional training unit to take our monthly probationary training exams. Word of my arrest of the car thieves had reached the guys at the unit, and I had quite a good reception from them when I arrived to do the exam for that month. Many of them had never handled such a complex case. One detective sergeant in particular, Bob Giles, was very encouraging. 'That's a good job, mate,' he said when he saw me. From then on, we had a very good rapport. Bob was in the process of setting up a new unit called the crime desk at Islington. He said to me, 'Once your probation is over, come and join the crime desk.'

During the summer of 1984, I got a well-earned break from A Relief with a two-week attachment onto the Street Duties 2 unit. We were tasked to deal with overnight car part thefts from Lindsay Baines, the Ford car dealership on Highbury Corner. As this was before the days of CCTV, identifying the culprits required direct surveillance. 'Right,' our sergeant said. 'We're going to do this through an observation van.'

One of the other constables had an old, beat-up VW camper van – a real relic of a thing. We drove it over to Lindsay Baines' forecourt, set up our observation point and sat patiently. Within a short space of time, I noticed something outside.

'Hold on,' I said. 'I just saw someone duck behind a vehicle.'

'Are you sure?' the sergeant said. I immediately crept out the back of the VW and went around the corner. There he was, helping himself to some wheel trims. He saw me and started running. I chased him across Highbury Corner into Highbury Fields, where I rugby tackled him and brought him back to the other officers. It was quite exhilarating doing such an arrest – the kind of thing I grew up seeing on old cop shows like *Dixon of Dock Green* or *Z Cars*! We found the stolen vehicles and again cleared up a good number of unsolved offences.

The manager of the dealership was over the moon. The thefts had caused him a lot of trouble, and he'd had their area manager pressuring him to ensure they stopped. He was so grateful, he offered me a special discount if I was looking to buy a car. I took him up on his kind offer; it helped me buy our first brand new vehicle, a Ford Fiesta.

'Well done,' Bob said the next time he saw me. 'You are definitely coming to the crime desk when you finish your probation.'

Sergeant Taplin, on the other hand, wasn't as congratulatory – especially when I showed up with a brand new car. 'Where did you get the money for that?' he demanded.

'I used to work before I joined this job,' I replied. 'I'm not on the take, if that's what you're thinking.'

I didn't have to tell him how I got a discount for the car. But he couldn't believe that I could afford it. Having my own work colleagues make such assumptions about me made me think that there was a good chance they would make similar assumptions with people on the street too – especially people who looked like me. It was discouraging, but I knew that I was in the Met for a reason; to challenge those assumptions.

I got through my probation pretty smoothly, even though I had challenges from the other guys. In the end they came around. I did a bit of boxing, and they loved me for that. I wasn't very good, but I was able to represent the division at the Met's annual amateur boxing championship, the Lafone Cup. I didn't do very well, but at least I tried. I was fit, but boxing really wasn't in my nature. I'm not into inflicting pain on people for sport. For me, participating in boxing events was simply a means of showing that I could survive, even if I took myself out of my comfort zone and offset the assumptions of my white colleagues.

Before I knew it, I was ending my probation. Again, Bob Giles said, 'At the end of your probation, do you want to join the crime desk?'

'Yes, but someone has to talk to Sergeant Taplin,' I said.

'Don't worry, I'll deal with it, because I have the backing of the Divisional top team to form this unit of active and effective officers, and you are on my list.' he replied.

So, when Bob Giles invited me on to a two-week attachment that ended up in a full-time role, not even Sergeant Taplin could reverse it, regardless of how much he put the fear of God into the inspector. Sergeant Taplin wasn't actually in charge of A Relief; an inspector was. But the inspector just did whatever Sergeant Taplin said. It was a rather odd case of reverse management, the sergeant controlling the inspector, but it happened because the sergeant was the more experienced and was feared by so many people.

Not all cases of reverse management were down to experience, though; some happened for more sinister reasons. I remember there was a PC at King's Cross – a crime prevention officer – who had massive influence on officers senior to him. I noticed that whenever he would come into the station, senior officers would suddenly straighten up and almost jump to attention in a form of reverence, an acknowledgement of the high esteem he was held in. 'He's only a PC like me,' I'd think to myself. 'Why does everyone respond in that way whenever he walks in?' I found out he was very high up in the Masonic Lodge. 'Hmm,' I thought.

That wasn't my first brush with Freemasonry in the organization. The next one happened on the Hendon athletics field, of all places, years later when I was a sergeant in Hackney. Someone came up to me after I'd won the 110 metre hurdles at Hendon and popped a booklet in my hand. 'It would be good if you read this,' he said. The booklet was on the 'Brotherhood'. It was basically a recruiting pamphlet for the Freemasons. I handed it back to him and said, 'Sorry, I'm not interested.'

My rejection of all things to do with Freemasonry was set in the late 1960s, when my Dad had a major rift with an in-law who tried to recruit him into Freemasonry, because it went against my Dad's principles of a meritocracy. I remember him passionately emphasizing to me that he wouldn't be in any way involved with any secret organization, where members helped each other at the expense of equality and justice.

Throughout my time in the Met, I always heard it whispered that joining the Freemasons was a sure way of fast-tracking my career, but it wasn't the way I wanted to do it. I didn't want to be beholden to anyone. It became clear when I dug deeper that people knew it was endemic in the organization, the elephant in the room, casting a huge shadow over police transparency. I thought, 'That's going to be another challenge; apart from the colour of my skin.' But I prefer being my own person, and not ingratiating myself in something I suspected had sinister foundations. In the police service, it helps if you have allies. I think that's why the Freemasons are so strong: your 'brothers' are supposed to be your allies. I wasn't going to advance my career through those means. I would do it through my own skills and abilities. My attitude was that I was going to make my way up the ranks through my own merits, taking the opportunities that I felt were the right things to do at the time. The crime desk posting was a seamless way to end my two-year probationary period and remove the shackles of Taplin, and the other A Relief sergeants. They tried to pull me back, but Bob Giles wouldn't have it and kept me on the new unit. If you look at crimes as having levels or degrees of seriousness, then the crime desk was a first tier of sorts. We dealt with relatively minor crimes, as opposed to complex cases such as rapes, kidnappings or murders. Occasionally, some of the low-level crimes we investigated did lead us on to serious ones. If that happened on a crime you were investigating, the detective constables or detective sergeants would take you under their wing and allow you to follow it through. That really widened your scope as an officer. It made a difference from just dealing with drug possession or shoplifters etc, and allowed us to get our teeth into more complex investigations.

It might have been a coincidence but shortly after joining the crime desk, I got the cowardly calling card of the racist elements, with 'NIGGER' daubed on my locker door, within a secure part of the station. I wasn't surprised because I had heard of this happening before to other black officers. I reported it immediately to the station chief inspector, which didn't result in any meaningful investigation because a statement wasn't even taken from me and no suspects were identified. It wasn't taken seriously enough by some senior officers, who also allowed casual racist comments to take place without any disciplinary action being taken, allowing the occupational culture to be polluted with these vile comments and attitudes. I didn't know how or when it would happen, but I sensed this form of casual racism would come to an end and I wouldn't dwell on it. Instead, I would make the most of this new phase in my career.

I was enjoying myself so much working on the crime desk, I came to the attention of the superintendent, Hugh Kinlock. Because the crime desk was a new unit, Hugh took a lot of interest in it. Hugh was a real Scottish gent, a good thinker and a decent man. He was stern; he never ingratiated himself with people or tried to be Mr Popular. He gave very clear leadership; he maintained a critical distance from junior members of the division. I think he used to like talking to me because he'd heard about my science background. I saw him as someone I could model myself on.

One day Hugh was walking by the crime desk and we struck up a conversation. He hadn't really heard of me, other than that I was the only black officer on the division. He didn't know how old I was (by this time, I was 28). He thought I was a bit younger. Nevertheless, the discourse we had was quite mature. I told him my background and the challenges I'd had with the police as a youngster; about what happened with my dad and how it almost stopped me from joining the organization. I think he was really caught by the story – by me still joining the police despite all that.

During my time on the crime desk, Hugh asked me to be his staff officer on large scale public order duties. If he was selected to be a senior command officer at Notting Hill Carnival, Remembrance Day or the Trooping of the Colour etc, I would be his runner. If a superintendent chooses you to be their runner, that's a clear sign that superintendent holds you in high esteem. They've chosen you because of your calibre, character and the chemistry between the two of you; it's a sign that they feel they can rely on you; that you can work unsupervised and even speak on their behalf when they're not around to speak for themselves. Invariably, that sort of job would be allocated to a more experienced constable, colloquially known as the 'Old Sweat'. I only had about two and half years' service when Hugh chose me to be his runner, so unsurprisingly, it didn't go down well with my peers. A role like that normally goes to a seasoned officer who has been there 15 or 20 years – not someone who's only been there 30 months!

Some officers thought I was getting favourable treatment because I was black. But Hugh Kinlock was not that sort of person. I believe he chose me because I knew certain parts of London very well, including Notting Hill. Hugh used to be one of the sector commanders in charge of policing the Notting Hill Carnival, and he felt I would add value because of my cultural understanding as a Londoner who had enjoyed carnival in the past. I guess the people who were upset expected me to turn down Hugh's offer, but there was no way I was going to turn down an opportunity to learn directly from one of the more forward-thinking senior officers.

Meanwhile, Sergeant Taplin was trying his hardest to get me back onto A Relief. But I stayed put. I was investigating crimes and getting really good results; I had a lot of clear-ups and gathered a lot of intelligence for the intelligence unit, known as the collator's office at the time. The crime desk was mainly a 'uniform' job, but we did do some undercover work.

It wasn't long before my cultural awareness of London was rewarded by my secondment onto the Homicide Investigation Team for the Stockwell Strangler case: a series of murders committed in south London between April and July 1986.

The killer's first victim was a 78-year-old former schoolteacher, Nancy Emms, who was found dead in bed in her flat in Wandsworth. At first everyone thought she had died of natural causes. Then Nancy's home help pointed out her television was missing, which meant she could have been burgled. A post-mortem was carried out, and it revealed Nancy had not only been murdered; she had also been sexually assaulted.

Two months later, on 9 June, another woman was found strangled in another flat in Wandsworth. Then on 28 June, two elderly Polish men were murdered at a residential home in Stockwell. Investigating officers found a palm print on one of the windows at the scene of the second murder. This was very quickly identified as belonging to a previously convicted burglar called Kenneth Erskine.

We now had a suspect. Erskine was a young man of mixed heritage, in his early twenties. He clearly researched his victims and the premises he burgled; he always went for somewhere owned by an elderly person. He was very ruthless in that regard. One of the first things the crime desk noticed was that the murders all seemed to take place along the Victoria Line, and so I was dispatched to Brixton to do some inquiries. We finally found the suspect and he was arrested on 27 July – at the dole office on Keyworth Street in Elephant and Castle, where he'd been signing on since 1984. He was taken to Clapham Police Station, where Fred Prentice (a pensioner from Clapham, who was the only one of his victims fortunate enough to survive) picked him out of an identity parade.

When the case came to the Old Bailey, I was attached to one of the exhibits officers. I've always been interested in the role exhibits play in painting a picture of what's happened in a case; I guess forensics appealed to my linear thinking as a scientist. One of my initial ambitions when I became a cop was to be a forensic lab sergeant, but the Home Office made it a role for civilians. Helping with the exhibits on the Stockwell Strangler case was the closest I ever got to being a lab sergeant. I savoured the opportunity, especially knowing it secured a conviction and took a serial killer off the streets.

The trial began on 12 January 1988 and ended on 29 January. It was my first time going to the Old Bailey, and I couldn't believe I was there in such a short space of time. Many officers never get to go there, yet here I was, with about three years in service, assisting the investigators. The Old Bailey is steeped in history, since it has been London's Central Criminal Court since the seventeenth century. It was an amazing feeling, being there as an investigator. The trial itself gave me much to ponder. 'What created that mindset where you have to take people's lives?' You just realize that anyone could be capable of anything.

I realized very quickly that I would have to absorb information like a sponge. All police officers do, of course, but something about this particular case really brought home to me how vital it was. It also taught me the importance of the role of officers and public servants, and the purpose of law and order. Justice has to be seen to be done, regardless of a person's circumstances. We are the executors of the justice system that demands our total accountability and transparency.

Career-wise, I had no doubts the experience I'd gained from my involvement in the case would stand me in good stead for future CID development. It was essential in that era to have a good reputation when you went for the next role, whether it was for a specialism or promotion. Having experience of working on such a high-profile murder investigation, when I'd only been on the force for three years, could only help my career prospects. Or so I thought...

I set about acquiring a lot of operational experience in the following months, and then put in an application to join the CID.

There were three positions open, which five candidates applied for. I knew I was a very strong candidate. I was the youngest in service by far; the others had done about double my service time, if not triple – some had done ten years. I did what I felt was a very strong interview, only to find all three positions were filled and I wasn't one of them. I went to the detective chief inspector for some feedback, and I couldn't believe my ears when he said, 'Your face didn't fit.'

'Because I'm black?'

'Oh – no, no, no.'

This was the first time I'd felt the need to challenge senior officers, and I wasn't convinced by the DCI's reply. One of the other candidates had come out of his interview and boasted that he'd lied through his teeth throughout. I mentioned this – without naming the person – and said, 'This officer came out here, and admitted that he lied.'

'I knew he was lying,' the DCI replied. 'But bullshit baffles brains.'

'Is that how it works?' I thought. 'Well, if this is what the CID is about, I want nothing to do with it.'

'You can stuff the CID,' I said. 'If I'm going to continue on here, I'll always be a uniformed officer.' I promptly walked out, turning my back on the CID and never looked back,

I have no regrets, because I saw how other colleagues of mine tried time and time again to get into the CID. There was one guy I knew from school. I bumped into him during my first week at Hendon; he was in his eighteenth week by then, nearly at the end of his 20-week training. We kept in touch; he was in a different borough, but we'd see each other from time to time. Over a ten-year period, he applied repeatedly to join the CID but could never get in, to his intense frustration. There's no way I could tread water for that amount of time. In hindsight, maybe telling that DCI to stuff his job wasn't that wise a move. In the

Met, rumours precede you. I can just picture the other officers saying, 'Logan's at it again.'

***

I stayed at the crime desk for about another year, but after that interview I knew I couldn't stay there permanently. Fortunately for me, Hugh Kinlock came along with a tantalizing offer.

'I'm setting up a divisional intelligence unit and I'd like you to be part of it,' he said. 'You can shape it however you want.'

The unit was to be at divisional HQ at King's Cross, and I would be working with Sergeant Bob Giles – the same detective who had got me onto the crime desk. That in itself was a good enough reason to say yes. Bob was a transformational, innovative and very supportive supervisor.

My job title was divisional research officer. I did research around how the borough division was seen to be performing in comparison with other boroughs within the Met. What types of crimes were being reported? How many of those were being solved? What was the clear-up rate? How were we perceived by the public? How many public complaints were we getting? Computers were becoming a big part of our daily work; back then in the late 1980s, they were the ones with horrible green screens and lines and lines of text. They didn't do my eyesight much good, and at the ripe old age of 30, I began wearing spectacles; middle age was kicking in fast!

Working at the intelligence unit was like being back in the lab. Being a scientist is good preparation for being a policeman; it sets you up with some excellent transferrable skills. As a scientist, you cannot make assumptions; you have to go by empirical evidence and be as objective as possible when approaching a problem. It's like a chemical reaction: you need to notice each stage as it comes, or have an idea of what you're looking for. In a lot of ways, that's how a police officer should deal with a criminal investigation: you have to go where the evidence takes you and not fall into the trap of assuming someone is guilty because of their class, colour, lifestyle or faith etc. And you can't not deal with them properly, if they are the victims of crime, because of their backgrounds. I know Hugh recognized that I had developed a knack for analytical thinking from my background in science, and it was not him being tokenistic. Nor was it the fact that we shared the same name, as some of my colleagues suggested. Just in case you hadn't figured it out, my middle name is Hugh: a reflection of my Scottish heritage.

Peter Imbert (later Lord Imbert) served as commissioner of the Met from 1987 to 1993. When he started in the role, he came to King's Cross to see our divisional intelligence unit. He said something quite profound: 'If all you officers are in the office gathering all this information, how many of you are on the street to act on it?' That struck a chord with me; I was aware that sometimes we had more analysts than street patrollers, and we needed to keep the right balance. I guess that's how lots of intelligence analysts became police staff members, so we weren't using officers to do the number-crunching. We must have been really cutting edge if the commissioner was coming to see what we were doing.

Predictably, my being asked to be a part of this unit upset some people. But I thought, if I'm unpopular I don't mind, as long as it's for the right reasons. Hugh really turned my thoughts around in regard to investigating the wider community, and thinking strategically about how you engage with communities. He was a good mentor.

One day, Hugh called me into his office. I felt a little nervous as he shut the door, sat down behind his desk and gave me a hard stare. What had gone wrong? Hugh sensed my unease and grinned. 'You should think about promotion,' he said.

I'd only been in the Met almost four years by this time. 'I'm a bit young in service,' I said.

'How old are you?'

'Thirty.'

'You're not young,' said Hugh. 'You've got a lot of life skills to bring into the organization. You've got a lot of experience, and you've crammed a lot in three-and-a-bit years. Go for it.'

There has been a lot of research showing that people from minority groups hold themselves back in work situations, believing they're not qualified, or that they haven't got the ability, to go for senior positions. Sometimes we feel we need to be twice as qualified or twice as experienced to even imagine we can compete with our white counterparts, whereas our white counterparts appear to think: 'I'm qualified by the fact that I'm confident in myself.' This approach needs to be backed up by evidence of their achievements.

To prepare for the promotion, I had to go to evening classes – which, in those days, involved memorizing more A reports. We had to know the instruction manual back to front. The manual came in the form of a black binder with removable sections. Each time a law was changed, or some policy modified, you'd be sent the relevant updated sections and you'd remove the old section from your binder and replace it with the most current copy. We were constantly amending sections in our manuals.

I wanted to supplement my learning with ongoing practical experience, and so I took up a community cop – Home Beat – role for the Barnsbury area close to Caledonian Road. Parts of Barnsbury reminded me of Dickens' *A Tale of Two Cities*. You had places such as the Canonbury area, where you would see some of the most expensive houses in London, on the same street as some of the most run-down estates. For me, being a community officer meant recognizing the importance of relationships, and being there for people. Treating people with respect and dignity was key, regardless of their circumstances. I would always remember the Beatitudes: sons and daughters of God are meant to keep the peace – and according to our oath, police officers are meant to keep the Queen's peace. Working in Islington ignited a desire in me to know how you worked with communities in a way that was relationship-based. That always was a theme throughout my service, and it continues to be in retirement.

On the evening of Wednesday 18 November 1987, I was at the top of Pentonville Road when I noticed a billowing cloud of smoke coming from King's Cross Station. I could see the smoke rising and then, as patrol officers, we got the message to go into the control room at the station and to remain on standby.

While we were on standby for hours, we heard the number of victims steadily increasing: one, then ten… all the way up to 100 injured and 31 fatalities. The deceased included one of the firefighters dispatched to put out the fire. I felt a sense of utter helplessness, dread and despair that day. We knew that the British Transport Police were there – the firefighters were too – but when we went to the station and started to see the death toll rise, it was just devastating.

Then we wondered what could have set it off. Was it an incendiary device? We eventually learned that it was an accident; a lit match had dropped onto a wooden escalator, and it went up like a torch.

As a cop, one thing you can't afford to do in such a situation is internalize your feelings about what has happened. You've got to come out of yourself and be a source of confidence and reassurance for people, and give them the sense that you're there for them. I tried to do that as best as I could, but it was hard.

If you go to King's Cross Station today, you can see the plaque erected in memory of the people who died in the fire. I will never forget that night, especially the overpowering smell of acrid smoke. It was devastating to know that so many people perished and there was nothing we could do. That much loss is hard to handle, especially when it's on your doorstep.

After I went for the promotion and got through, I found myself, ironically, in an acting sergeant's role on A Relief, the team I started in. They always put me in the custody suite to book in prisoners. I could have requested a move to another team, but I didn't. Some officers did leave; some sergeants did too – including the dreaded Sergeant Taplin. I spent about eight months in that role. When I was eventually made a sergeant, those eight months proved to have been invaluable in preparing me to be a sergeant. I'd learned how to book prisoners in, how to do briefings/debriefings and to supervise officers and give them guidance around all sorts of situations in and out of the station.

They do say that this first promotion – going from constable to sergeant – is the biggest jump a cop can make. It's your first supervisory role, and you cannot afford to be seen as a 'constable with stripes'. You have to maintain that critical distance. You have to show ethical leadership. You have to show professionalism. You have to look the part; you have to lead by example and be there in a supportive way for your team. Especially as a sergeant, it's what you don't do that invariably comes back to haunt you.

The only other ethnic minority officer I came across during my time in Islington during this last phase was Dal Babu, who was with me at Hendon, and who I have mentioned before. He had been a teacher before joining the Met, and he still cared very much about young people – which was why he'd joined the Youth and Community Section based in the same building. Before I left on promotion, we would reminisce about our time at Hendon, with a joint sense of achievement for having survived our first five years, despite the challenges of the occupational culture that was continuously more hostile for minority ethnic officers. We shared an unspoken agreement to keep looking forward, by developing our careers and taking pride in being role models for our communities. Almost forty years later, we are still friends, having risen through the ranks and both retiring in 2013. We are still active members of our communities, which shows public service is not a tap you can just switch off, especially when people need your help.

5

Joy and pain

Five years after joining the Met, I was posted to Edmonton as a
sergeant in the autumn of 1988. Compared to Islington – where
I'd grown up and knew the area inside out – working in Edmonton was like being transplanted into a different county.

All of a sudden, I was now a supervisor and had to make sure
I showed the right sort of leadership. Telling people what to do
can make you unpopular. There was also the extra barrier of
being a black supervisor. There would always be that one person who reckoned you only got the job because of your colour.
The fact that I had previously been a scientist also made some
people suspicious of me – as did the notion that I was doing this
because I believed I had a calling to become a cop. I did have a
faith, but at that time it was one with a small 'f', so to speak. I
wasn't a committed Christian then, but even so, I could see the
importance of holding close to my convictions. But whether it
had a big F or a small one, my faith was tested daily. Being a
new sergeant was like being a new recruit – like going from primary school to secondary school. I was now a supervisor as well
as a new officer on my block, and there weren't that many black
supervisors.

One of the things you learn as a police officer is coping, and
one way of doing that for me was to give the best service that
I could. Every now and then, someone who I knew personally
would ask me to assist with some police issue they had, but I
tried to keep that to a minimum – not because I was trying to
cocoon my family from the realities of police life; it was just that

I didn't want my work to have a ripple effect on my private life. That wouldn't have been fair on Gretl or our children. Home should be as calm, loving and nurturing as possible.

I distinctly remember one incident that happened when I was six months into my promotion. I was on night duty. As a newly promoted sergeant, you spend much of your time on night shifts and late turn shifts, booking in prisoners. You could easily spend an entire shift doing that. Normally, I would go to the locker room, put my things away and then enter the custody suite via the staff entrance. On this particular evening, I was running a bit late. I didn't want to hold up the late turn officer, so instead of going into the locker room as usual, I went in by the front entrance instead, ready to take over from the late turn and get stuck in right away. As I was going through the station office, I noticed that it was full of concerned looking parents. The custody suite was also full of young people – some as young as 13.

'What's going on?' I asked the late turn.

He explained that the local Robbery Squad had been working in the area. Gangs had started to commit muggings and robberies en masse on public transport, where their potential victims were hemmed in – a practice that had come to be known as 'steaming'. This unit had been following a group of young people involved in steaming on buses and in transport hubs, starting in Hackney, then in Haringey and finally in Enfield. The correct police procedure is that you're supposed to arrest someone as soon as you see them committing an offence. Instead of doing that, this squad had continually watched these people commit a string of offences – all the way from Hackney and a few miles up to Edmonton, where they finally arrested them.

'Who's the officer on the case?' I asked.

'A detective inspector.'

'Where is the officer now?'

'Oh, he's gone for the night.'

'What do you mean?'

'They were under the impression that you would authorize their detention until the following morning for interviews.'

'Oh, were they?' I said. 'I'm just supposed to rubber-stamp this and let these youngsters stay in the cells until they decide to come back in the morning?'

As far as I was concerned, the arrests had not been carried out expeditiously. So the first thing I needed to do was to get the officers on the case back into the station to explain to me why they couldn't carry out their interviews immediately, especially if they had *prima facie* evidence. I had a station full of irate parents, and some of these youngsters were under 15. Unless something critical was happening, there was no way I was going to authorize the detention of 13-year-olds when I could release them into the custody of their parents and they could come back in the morning – which, to me, was the most humane way of dealing with the situation. There was also the Police and Criminal Evidence (PACE) Act 1984 code of conduct to consider.

The late turn didn't agree with my assessment of the situation, but as he was now off duty and I was the custody officer, I was the one who had to deal with it.

One of my fellow sergeants, Andy McKechnie, came in and I explained what the late turn had handed over to me, with the assumption that I was going to let the youngsters wallow in the cells overnight. I told Andy I wasn't going to do that, and he was in total agreement with me. From my experience on the crime desk, I observed specialist CID officers, like the Flying Squad, assume uniformed officers would just do whatever they told us to. I was the last person to be railroaded by the CID and so they weren't going to dictate to me; I was going to comply with PACE. I decided I was going to call the arresting officer back in to clear up his own mess.

The detective inspector didn't turn up, but the detective sergeant did. He was about to have a drink with some of the rest of his squad in a nearby pub around the corner. I called my duty inspector and told him what I was going to do. 'Do it,' he said. 'You're the custody officer.'

Some of the children the squad had arrested reminded me of myself. For a start, every single one of them was black. I could easily have been in their position if I had been in the wrong peer group. I had two young children myself, and that made me think that in a few years' time, it could be them caught up in a mess like this.

The detective sergeant turned up at around a quarter to eleven. 'Sergeant, I hear there's a bit of a problem,' he said.

'I haven't got a problem,' I replied, 'but you might have.'

'Why's that?' he asked.

'I've got a room full of parents wanting to know what's happened to their children. Your team followed these youngsters for hours, and then arrested them between three and four in the afternoon. What have you been doing with them all this time?'

'We've been getting statements from victims.'

'You must have quite a few, because you allowed these youngsters to run around Hackney, Haringey and Enfield. In all honesty, you've ended up with the wrong custody sergeant here, because you are going to interview all the ones who are under 17.'

'But that's five of them!'

'Yes and afterwards I'll make a decision as to what happens next. In the meantime, I will review the others. You'd better crack on.'

He was not happy. The rest of the squad were told in no uncertain terms that they were to remain on duty and report back to the station to work. On presenting themselves at the station, I could see in their faces that they weren't my biggest fans. None of that mattered to me. I knew I was doing the right thing, and I was not going to be deterred, rushed or coerced. I was determined to make a stand against misplaced loyalties. My role might have been a junior one – I'd only been a supervisor for six months – but I was not going to budge on this.

In the end, the team conducted five interviews, which they completed around three in the morning. Out of the total group, I released eight. Three required no further action. When the squad cast their net, they'd caught everyone in sight – including a few who were just in the wrong place at the wrong time and hadn't actually been involved. Five were bailed to return in the morning with their parents. The ones around 17 were quite hardened, and it was better to deal with them more thoroughly in the morning (interestingly, none of their parents were there). I spoke to the parents that were there; many of them were shocked and surprised but also grateful that an officer had taken the time to explain things to them – and, most importantly, let them take their children home.

After that night shift incident, I was Public Enemy Number 1 – plus plus – with certain members of the Flying Squad. I am relatively calm about it now, but at the time it tested every fibre of my being.

I knew the events of the night shift were going to come up when the superintendent called me into his office when I resumed my day shift a few days later. He wanted to know my rationale, and I explained clearly where I stood. In my head, I could still see the appreciative looks on the faces of the parents who'd been waiting all night for their children. If I had done something wrong, the uniformed superintendent or my duty officer would have spoken to me at the time, but they hadn't. I knew I'd upset the Flying Squad, but it had to be done. I heard the detective inspector was not impressed that his detective sergeant and some of his detective constables had been made to come back and interview the youngsters, but I said that although they weren't breaching PACE, they had stretched it to the extent that it was going to snap – and I was not going to allow that to happen.

'I totally agree with you, and your actions didn't compromise the case,' the superintendent said. 'Thank you very much.'

'Thank you, sir,' I said, and walked out.

That first real test as an officer, standing up for the rights of other people, gave me a greater sense of purpose. It made the calling of policing make more sense to me. I was able to assist those who needed an understanding of what was going on. I could understand the parents' plight because I was a parent myself, especially given our shared common experience as African Caribbeans. I never saw any of those parents again after that, but I can still see the looks in their eyes when I released their children back into their custody. I believe most of those youngsters went into court and half were found guilty, but at least I knew that the ones who were innocent were able to deal with that a bit better, having not been kept in overnight.

While all this was going on, my dad's assault was coming to the top of the list for civil action – seven years after the assault had taken place. This would be another test. I was still young in service as a sergeant.

I had deliberately avoided any possible interaction with those officers involved in my dad's case. I knew they were based at Holloway Police Station, where my parents lived. Back then, the borough was divided into two, with Holloway at the top and King's Cross at the bottom, with separate radio channels that were linked centrally in emergencies. Unintentionally I may have worked with these officers on policing a football match or a public march or demo, but I wouldn't have known them unless they introduced themselves to me – and no one ever did, which was fine by me. It would have been quite an awkward introduction: 'Hi, I once beat up your dad!'

I agreed without hesitation when Dad asked me to accompany him to court. I knew I would be of greater assistance to him from within the organization, rather than outside. And it would give me a chance to see which officers had assaulted him, having gone out of my way to avoid our paths crossing prior to this case.

On the day of the court case, I obtained authority to attend in uniform. The court was a county court in central London. I saw the officers – a sergeant and two constables – and they saw me. The fact that I was now a sergeant gave Dad a real sense of pride. Out of the blue, the clerk of the court informed us that the police had withdrawn their case. They accepted liability and there would be a full apology and financial compensation. It wasn't a finding of guilt, but rather proof that Dad was the victim of excessive force and unlawful arrest. The amount wasn't huge, but for Dad it was more about the principle. My being by Dad's side was a way of restoring some of the closeness we'd lost over those previous seven years, because of his concerns over my joining the organization whose members had assaulted him. I intentionally hugged my father in the public lobby so that the officers would see, to send a strong signal of solidarity, and we both left the courts with our heads held even higher.

***

One of the inspectors at Edmonton was looking for ways the police could engage with young people, and he recruited me as a sergeant, and three constables, to set up the Edmonton Volunteer Cadet Corps. I was far from being his first choice, because more experienced sergeants had turned down the opportunity, but I snapped it up. The concept was basically a police equivalent of the army cadets. I was thrilled to be asked, as this fitted well with my desire to work with young people, as I had done in Islington. I'd always loved outdoor activities as a Boy Scout, so this was playing to my strengths.

We recruited youngsters in the local area: 15 to 16-year-olds from a range of ethnicities and backgrounds. We made them aware of police powers and procedures; we also taught them first aid and orienteering, via the Duke of Edinburgh's Award scheme. We took them up to the Police Cadet unit in north Wales, near Snowdonia. Sometimes the cadets would be alongside officers policing sporting events, festivals, fetes and outdoor exhibitions. Part of our thinking was that if any of the youngsters had a calling for policing themselves, the corps would serve as a halfway house. It was quite a busy time for me; sometimes I would be on relief work and then I'd be going on one of these activities with the cadets. I often had to change my duties to make time to accompany the cadets.

The first time I was in charge of a group was when the cadets went on a week-long trip to Snowdonia. Our inspector had suffered a long-term illness, so I was left in charge of the constables and cadets. I had some really good, qualified staff with experts in mountaineering and orienteering. Jim Cline was one of our physical training instructors. He was really positive. We became great friends; he taught me how to ski and gave me an alpine skiing jacket, which I still wear to this day.

We had a good team spirit. For one of the adventures, we took the most difficult route up Snowdon: the route known as the Zigzags, part of the Pyg track. We had really capable mountaineers on the staff team, including Jim Cline, and they'd drilled the cadets well beforehand. We put two of our strongest mountaineers at the front, two at the back, and me in the middle. Snowdonia is the type of place where if the clouds suddenly descend, you cannot see more than a few feet ahead of you. Sure enough, as we ascended, a cloud enveloped us as we approached the summit.

The cloud only obscured our view for an hour, but that hour felt like a week. I was more scared than I've ever been in my life. Here I was with 18 youngsters in my care, and I couldn't see a thing. It was literally a couple of feet either way, and if you slipped, you'd drop 150 feet. I kept thinking, 'If anything goes wrong, I want to go too. How will I explain this to their parents?' I've dealt with risky situations in my career, but nothing like this. When the cloud eventually lifted, we were near the peak. From there, we joined a pathway and had a nice meandering walk back to base camp.

This short episode showed how well-trained young people could act as a team and not panic. The cadets revealed how well-drilled and disciplined they were. For me, it was a lesson in keeping your composure, especially when dealing with young people, who would have picked up any concerns and become agitated or fearful themselves. They want to know that you're in command, and you can take unforeseen circumstances in your stride. My mantra was 'It's not only about what happens to you in life, but how you deal with it.'

In 1989, Edmonton Police Station moved from the rickety old building on Fore Street that had been its home since 1916, to a modern eight-storey red brick building further up towards Edmonton Green. In those days, the Met was divided into eight areas, and the new station was to be the headquarters for 1 Area. All the senior managers were there – assistant commissioner, deputy assistant commissioners, commanders, chief superintendents – and they all knew me on first name terms. There weren't any other black sergeants, and I was in charge of the cadet corps, so all the senior officers knew me because they kept meeting me at different events. They'd pass me in the corridor and say, 'Hey Leroy, how's it going? How are the cadets?'

I started to get a certain amount of animosity from my other sergeants, but I thought, 'Come on, guys. None of you wanted to start it up, but now it's a success; I'm on the receiving end of your jealousy!'

This all came to a crescendo when we heard that HRH Princess Diana was going to open the new station. I had seen the princess before, during my time at Islington. She was a patron of Sadler's Wells Theatre in Rosebery Avenue, which was near to my Barnsbury community cop beat, and she was always there with the Queen Mother. I was proud to be part of the 'Thin Blue Line', together with a few other community colleagues to ensure they enjoyed their visits safely. All the same, it was still an amazing honour when she asked to meet my team of cadets.

As I was in charge of the cadets and staff, this immediately meant that I would be involved in the planning meetings, which took place in the conference room on the top floor of the building. I'd be in these meetings, and you would see all the chief superintendents and chief inspectors looking at me, wondering who this sergeant was and why he had such a prominent role to play. It was simple, really: I was there because Princess Diana had a real heart for young people and she wanted to know what the police were doing for them, especially when the cadets were seen as a community success that showed the police in a good light.

The day of the opening was a gloriously sunny day. Getting the youngsters prepared for it was a challenge, especially trying to contain their excitement. Diana was delayed getting to us, and the cadets were getting restless, all eager to show her everything they'd learned and, of course, to tell her about their mountaineering adventure in Wales. In the end, she turned up 25 minutes later than scheduled. As she walked into the conference room, I went up to meet and greet her and she said, 'I apologize for being late.' What do you say to a tardy princess? I couldn't exactly say, 'Well, don't do it again!'

'It's not a problem,' I said. 'Everyone's been looking forward to meeting you.'

The first thing I realized about Princess Diana was that her pictures did not do her credit. She had such beautiful features and was very humble, really down to earth with the cadets. She asked genuine questions, and showed real concern and interest. She'd been delayed getting to us as she had been visiting a hospice for youngsters. She was only supposed to spend 15 minutes with the cadets, but ended up spending 35 minutes with them. I could see her people outside the conference room glaring at us and tapping their watches. I had to jump in while she was asking the youngsters some questions. 'Ma'am, I hate to interrupt,' I said, 'but you need to move to another area because you've got the rest of the police station to get to.'

The opening ceremony was a grand, colourful event. There were stalls in the yard and members of the public were invited to come and see the building. I really felt that this was what a police station should be: an open, joyful place where people felt secure. Yes, part of a police station's purpose is to apprehend people. But another main focus is being there to help people, and the organization really should put greater emphasis on the pastoral aspects through sustainable and meaningful relationship building.

The cadets, staff and I received excellent feedback on how we represented both 1 Area HQ and the wider Metropolitan Police Service, especially from Princess Diana's representatives. It didn't stop there, because within a few weeks I was selected to attend a newly formed leadership course for supervisors. It was the inaugural course that mainly attracted senior leaders across the Met, and it wasn't a surprise for me to be the only African-Caribbean officer among thirty. I fully immersed myself in the five-day course because it played to my strengths by emphasizing more practical outward-bound team-building exercises and a minimum of class-based activities in the hilly Snowdonia terrain. I was already acquainted with this through recent work with my cadets.

On the penultimate day, we were surprised by the guest appearance of Commander John Grieve, the course coordinator, who was the head of the CID School and one of the 'Top Techs' in the Met. As a forward-thinking, charismatic transformational leader, he commanded a great deal of respect. I found John to be a breath of fresh air, and I instantly identified with him. He didn't appear to take himself as seriously as other very senior officers often did. This made him approachable, which made people feel comfortable in his presence, especially with his sophisticated quick wit. I was on the receiving end of his one-liners when he joined me onboard my homemade winning raft, from the last team competition to construct and row across the small Welsh lake. As a member of the winning team, John ordered me to row him back across the lake and dutifully I complied. Mischievously, I decided to rock the rickety raft – made of wooden pallets and oil drums – halfway across, causing him to exclaim, 'Logan, this could be the end of your short career if I get wet, much less capsize.' Fortunately, we landed on the other side fine and dry, which he always reminded me of whenever our paths crossed over the subsequent 20 years – especially on the occasion when he helped to extend my career rather than shorten it.

The cadet corps had been going for about two years when I began to hear some ugly rumours that I was having an affair with one of the cadets. I couldn't believe it. I know people within the police culture can be envious and treacherous, but I never thought anyone would stoop so low. Someone told me I should watch my back, and I decided they had a point. Just before Christmas 1990, I approached my supervisor and said, 'I want to be transferred. What's the place with the largest number of vacancies?'

'Hackney', came the reply.

'Oh my gosh,' I thought.

I knew Hackney from my college days there. It didn't hold any fear for me, but I knew it would be challenging – after all, this was where someone had tried to stab me just because I'd told him not to litter the street!

Rather than apply for Hackney straight away, I considered some other options within Edmonton. The first thing that came to mind was Area Complaints: the people who investigate officers who have had complaints made against them, or who have breached some regulation or protocol or even the law. The Area Complaints team was based in the same building, and I knew all the senior officers and got on really well with them. I applied for Area Complaints full of confidence, but I didn't get the job. I heard that one of the unwritten criteria for joining was that you had to be in a lodge. I could never prove this, but I knew another person who applied at the same time as I did, who had just become a Freemason, and got the job, while I was shut out.

'When one door closes, another one opens,' I thought to myself. I decided then that it was best that I move on. The rumours about the cadets and me were getting really malicious. This is why so many people leave the organization, especially in the first few years; they get to a point where they simply cannot deal with it. There is a strong camaraderie and a great team work ethic there – but if you get on the wrong side of the barrack room lawyers, the atmosphere and culture can be really hostile and toxic. So having established that I was not going to get the Area Complaints job, I submitted my application for Hackney.

I sensed my small-minded critics within the station were even more incensed by my success in athletics, especially being the Met champion for the 110m hurdles in 1991, and running the 1 Area athletics team, who in turn won the Met Team Championship under my leadership. Again this brought me to the attention of senior officers for being a positive representative for 1 Area.

This was even more reason for my cadets to get very upset when they heard I was leaving. They couldn't believe it, but I couldn't tell them why I'd decided to leave. Putting on the bravest face I could muster, I said to them, 'I've been a sergeant here for three years. I've got to move on.'

My leaving function was an emotional event. Even Gretl commented, 'The cadets are really sad you're leaving, aren't they?' It wasn't just the cadets and I who were moved that day; I had some great relationships with other staff members, people who would become long-term friends.

At Hackney, I was back in the custody suite – only this time, it was ten times as busy as the one at Edmonton. We dealt with really hard-nosed major crimes: murders, kidnappings and the like. I'd been involved in murder investigations before, but not as regularly as I was here – not to mention the frequent serious assaults and firearms investigations. It was a completely different world to Edmonton; you wouldn't believe it was just a few miles down the A10.

I was in the custody suite on one particularly horrible night shift, thinking to myself, 'Why did I leave Edmonton?' when the station officer called and said, 'You've got visitors.' This was about 11 o'clock at night – not the sort of time one expects visitors. As it turned out, the 'visitors' were some of my cadets from Edmonton: young men and women I'd first met when they were 14 and 15, who were now young adults. They had come to tell me that they missed me and that some of them were applying to become officers.

I couldn't believe my ears. It was a very busy shift that night, so I couldn't spend much time with them. But just having them drop by meant the world to me. I would meet up with them again from time to time after that; some of them went on to have 30-year careers in the Met.

To quote Frankie Beverly, my time at Edmonton was like sunshine and rain – a bittersweet experience. Some of it was painful, but some of it was joyful and very rewarding. Fortunately for me, the joyful elements outshone the painful ones.

6

Hackney (Round 1)

I could have fronted out the false accusations, but the truth is that as much as I liked Edmonton, I didn't find the job there demanding enough. I'd enjoyed starting up the cadet corps and I loved seeing them develop. But aside from that, the job really hadn't stretched me much.

Hackney, in contrast, was a hothouse of experience; so many people served there, it was like a masterclass in how to investigate crime. It was a non-stop borough; very diverse. A lot of people said, 'Why would you want to go there?' to which I would reply, 'Why not? I need something to get my teeth into that will take me out of my comfort zone, where I sharpen up my way of operating.'

I arrived at Hackney in October 1991 and joined the response team. We had an amazing inspector, Huw Jones. We used to call him the 'Ninja Inspector'. He was very active, enthusiastic, very articulate, a good planner and a good leader. He really set an example. I was pleased to be joining him, but the team was a tough one to control; it was full of strong characters. Quite a few of them kept testing me because I was a supervisor of colour. They knew I'd come from another station and so wasn't a newly made-up sergeant. Nevertheless, some of them saw I had come from a sleepy station and thought the three years I'd served in Edmonton didn't count for much. I had to prove myself constantly.

I only intended to stay at Hackney for three years, but you know what they say about the best laid plans. Owing to a moratorium on police pay and conditions aligned with the rank structure in the mid-1990s, there was a pause on promotions across the country for about three years. I saw it as an opportunity to develop my leadership skills by completing an external CIPD Human Resource course at the Holloway campus of Metropolitan University in Islington. I supplemented this with internal leadership courses to add to my portfolio, all the while making it very clear to everyone what my red lines were on clear professional and ethical principles. On the personal front, I was getting into books on leadership by Myles Munroe, a leading light in the international Pentecostal Church movement. He applied Christian principles to so many aspects of life in such a down to earth practical way. Even though I wasn't openly committed to my faith at that stage, his books planted seeds that germinated sooner rather than later.

It was my personal stance that kept me connected with the community, especially because Stoke Newington Police Station was perceived to have heavy-handed officers, to say the very least, by many in the black community. To this day, there are those who believe the police to have been the executioner of a black young man in the station office. It was in January 1983 – the year I joined the Met – that a 21-year-old black British man called Colin Roach died from a gunshot wound in the front office of Stoke Newington Police Station. Although that happened in the old listed building where the station was housed in 1983, its legacy lived on in the new building we were in now. The spectre of Colin Roach was always present. Community members and the media would mention him from time to time. The dub poet Linton Kwesi Johnson mentions him in his song 'Liesense fi Kill'. Sinead O'Connor's album *I Do Not Want What I Haven't Got* (the one with her cover of Prince's song 'Nothing Compares 2 U' on it) has a photograph of Colin's parents gazing mournfully at a poster of him. With that sort of legacy hanging over our heads, I firmly believed that we had to do things right and if not, to explain why not. We had to make sure we were extremely ethical to reassure the public, especially black people who historically lacked trust in the police. I could personally testify to that.

Another significant case that added to Stoke Newington's damaged reputation was commonly known as the 'Dalston Seven.' An investigation had started because exhibits kept going missing from serious criminal cases investigated by CID officers. It was alleged that a CID officer was seizing exhibits from crime scenes, but those exhibits could never be found. Cases were compromised because the evidence had disappeared. Even the local drug dealers were accusing the police of being dodgy. You'd be interacting with them – whether it was an arrest or not – and they'd say, 'Those Stoke Newington officers seized our drugs and our money', but there'd be no sign of either at the station.

In the end, the rumours turned into allegations and an internal investigation was carried out. Seven CID officers were suspended. One of them was an officer called Ronnie Palumbo. During the investigation, they found out that Ronnie had some underworld connections: his father-in-law, Kenneth Harris, had a previous conviction for supplying drugs through a truck haulage company he ran. In November 1995, a large quantity of cannabis was found hidden in the trailer of one of Harris's lorries at Dover docks. In court, it was revealed that the lorry had made four trips during the latter half of 1995 and that Ronnie had travelled out on all four trips. He and his father-in-law were jailed for a total of 41 years. 'It could only happen in Stoke Newington', I thought when I heard the news.

I knew of Ronnie Palumbo long before I actually met him. He was almost like criminal folklore in Hackney. They say there's a fine line between a good cop and a criminal, and

Ronnie embodied that. He had a good nose for sniffing out arrests. He just didn't know his boundaries and thought he was untouchable.

My time on A Relief at Hackney was very demanding, but I was enjoying working with a dynamic team. This didn't stop me from maintaining my love for athletics. I won the Met 110m hurdles a further couple of years in 1992 and 1993, as well as leading 1 Area to further success as Met Team Athletics Champions. I was still getting a buzz competing and beating guys almost half my age.

7

The birth of the BPA

In 1989, the Met's HR department acknowledged that it had a problem.

Fourteen years earlier, the then commissioner Sir Robert Mark had started a campaign for 'more police of colour in London'. Despite his efforts, not only had the organization remained low on black and Asian recruits, the majority of the few it did attract tended to quit within their first two years on the job.

Wyn Jones was now the Met's assistant commissioner in charge of recruitment and training. Not one to turn down a challenge, he took a radical step to deal with the problem. Wyn figured that the best way to find out why recruitment and retention of minority ethnic officers was so problematic would be to hear first-hand from those officers what their working lives were like. And so he decided to ask them. Every black and Asian officer received an invitation to meet at Bristol Polytechnic, in two-day syndicates. Everyone, that is, except me. Somehow my HR file had been changed – and so, according to the records, I was white! I called up Scotland Yard and said, 'I fit the criteria as a black officer, but I wasn't put on the list.'

At the same time, my white colleagues were concerned for what it was all about and what we would say about them, as if it could lead to disciplinary action for some people. I was as much in the dark as they were, and so I would glibly reply 'Watch this space.'

Eventually my invitation arrived in the summer of 1990, and I joined the other syndicate officers who filled a conference room in New Scotland Yard to be briefed on our visit to Bristol Poly-technic. I was aware of the format from earlier syndicate partic-ipants, and they warned me of the long drive in a basic 'no frills' bus, commonly known as a 'Green Goddess'. Surprise surprise: the racist elements in the Met renamed it the 'Wog Wagon to Bristol'. Even though it was never said to me directly, it had the same impact as 'Nigger' being written on my locker a few years earlier.

From the moment we stepped on the coach that took us to Bristol, it was evident that something special was brewing. The coach ride was peppered with animated conversations, and I really felt a sense of family among work colleagues that I hadn't met before. When we arrived at Bristol Polytechnic, I was amazed at how many other black officers there were. There were black chief inspectors, inspectors and sergeants like me. The camaraderie and the sense of togetherness among us was unforgettable, and we struck up lifelong friendships, not just professionally but personally, like the friendship I began with Shabnam Chaudhri. She ended up working with me operation-ally years later and proved to be a sound source of confidential advice, as well as a great mate socially in the local area of Essex where we both reside. We also shared a similar choice in soul music.

Over the following two days, we opened up our veins and bled out the pain we suffered in the hostile environment of the occupational culture. One officer told how whenever he would radio his colleagues, they would make monkey noises back at him. Every N-word we'd ever been subjected to while at work – be it in the staff canteen or on the football pitch – came out. For everyone who spoke, the experience was brave and soul-searching. Typically for me, I wasn't going to go through this process and then go back to business as usual. I didn't see Bristol as just a series of seminars; for me it was a call to action.

This drive for change energized me to successfully apply for a position on the working group tasked with writing up a report on the seminars.

During my time on the working group, it became clear that black police staff members had gone through a similar process and the emerging themes of the hostile environment they were experiencing was a mirror image of what we were going through as black police officers. It was obvious that black officers and police staff were stronger working together, to modernize the Met around race equality issues and stand up against injustices in this regard.

Our report on the Bristol Seminars was published in 1991 – but in fine Met tradition, it got shelved. Around the time it was due to come out, Wyn was subject to an inquiry of criminal misconduct that led to a special disciplinary tribunal, ultimately resulting in his dismissal for being unfit to hold office. The shadow of that tribunal cast an ominous shroud across all of his portfolios. Consequently, every project report he was involved in got sidelined – the Bristol Seminars being one casualty. However, those of us who had attended the seminars had no intention of abandoning what Wyn had set in motion. As members of the working groups, we started to host large scale social events called 'Bristol Reunions.' These quickly became highly anticipated dates, not only in the diaries of predominantly black personnel but also other black public servants from outside the Met, who were invited to attend, such as firefighters, health workers, teachers etc. The first event in 1991 set a high bar, with everyone dressed to impress in the main banqueting suite of the Strand Palace hotel, enjoying the positive vibe primarily created by the uniqueness of the occasion. Everyone was bright-eyed and bushy-tailed, networking in a different outward facing cultural way, with the wider community embracing us wholeheartedly in large numbers.

Things moved on a step over the next couple of years, with our reunions attracting larger numbers and gaining community prominence, even in the media, and we became a victim of our own success, which necessitated that we structured ourselves into an independent organization with a proper constitution. Consequently, in April 1993 – the same month that a young black man from south London called Stephen Lawrence was murdered – we started having meetings in Bessborough Place, next to Pimlico Underground station. I remember the first founder member meeting comprising of about 20 people – black officers and police staff – squeezed in the small meeting room, effervescent with expectation to own and act on the Bristol Seminar report. Uncharacteristically I didn't say anything, but continued to take in everything that was being agreed about structuring ourselves. After two hours, I was asked why I was so unnaturally quiet, to which I replied, 'I wonder how many of us will still be around in ten years' time?' It was a rhetorical question, not only about commitment but also regarding the hostility we were going to face for just existing. Right or wrongly, I knew I would be there.

We met monthly, under the initial guidance of DCI Mike Fuller, to formulate our constitution, with cutting edge aims and objectives for what would become the Met Black Police Association. While we were working on it, more details about Stephen's death emerged. They made for very depressing reading. However, thanks to our experiences on the job, none of it came as a surprise to us. We saw media reports saying that officers involved in the investigation knew the suspects' families; that people knew who did it and had passed that information on to the police, but somehow the investigating officers had not acted on any of the information they'd received. There were even suggestions at those early stages that the investigating officers were not merely incompetent but actually corrupt.

As 1994 dawned, we had to make a decision: what were we going to do? We now had a constitution, aims and objectives. Our mission was simple: we wanted to improve the working environment of black police officers and police staff, so that we were in a better position to serve the needs of the black community. We knew about the disproportionalities in stop and search and the force used in those encounters; we knew about the lack of trust and confidence that the black community had in the police in certain areas because of the heavy-handed treatment they'd experienced. We knew something needed to be done and we had to speak up.

News of our new group soon reached the ears of the Metropolitan Police Federation: the staff association of which every constable, sergeant, inspector and chief inspector in the Met is a member. We learned that the Federation was very angry when it heard about our meetings. A black police association wasn't needed, they claimed; rather than setting one up, we should just join the Federation. But we were already part of it – and it wasn't doing anything to help black officers, who suffered internally from a lack of promotion and were more likely to be disciplined. As a result, they were leaving the Met in disproportionate numbers. The Federation tried to intimidate us from an early stage. Unfortunately, from our core group of about 20 or so people, a few ran for cover.

Soon we established links with black officers in the USA, members of the National Black Police Association in Washington. Their executive director was Ron Hampton, a tall, dashing American with a silver beard and a stylish gold earring that really suited him. He was a retired officer by this time, having served about 25 years (American officers don't do the full 30 years' service British officers do). Ron was now the NBPA's ambassador, an outreach worker and trouble-shooter. He was well known in the press in the USA, and was a visiting lecturer at

Columbia University. He reminded me of Martin Luther King; he spoke eloquently like him, and even though he didn't use Bible references in the same way, he was jaw-dropping when he spoke like a preacher in the pulpit. He was six foot four, always immaculately dressed, and he appeared to walk effortlessly, giving the impression that he was gliding. You'd think he could walk on water, the way he hovered along.

When Ron was in London, he came to speak to us while we were agonizing over what to call ourselves. We were debating whether we should be the Black and Asian Police Association or the Black Minority Ethnic Police Association. 'Just call yourselves black,' he said. 'The term "black" has history; the struggle for equality and justice that goes all the way back to slavery.' He crystallized it in our minds and gave us a lot more confidence. This meant we defined the term 'Black' not as a reference to skin colour, but to the shared and common experience of those from African, African-Caribbean and Asian origins.

My world of operational work really took up a great deal of my attention, and I was also on a steep learning curve with my involvement in forming the BPA. Even though I'd been in the job for about ten years by this time, I was learning voraciously – too voraciously. I was so wrapped up in work, I didn't notice the warning signs that I wasn't giving home the amount of attention I should have.

Then, in November 1993, Gretl said she'd had enough, and she left me. We had three children by this time: Gerad was ten, Leah was seven and Myles was just coming up to his first birthday. I was devastated. Gretl took Myles with her and moved in with her sister.

'These things happen,' I thought to myself. 'I'll give her a bit of time; she just wants some space.' I thought she would come back for Myles's birthday later that month, but the birthday came and went, and she didn't return. Now I started thinking, 'This is serious.' I had the support of my parents; they helped me to make sure that Leah and Gerad were going to school and there was continuity in their lives, even though obviously they missed their mum. 'Your mum's going to come back,' I kept saying to them.

About the same time I successfully applied to be the divisional training sergeant. It was the first time I'd been off shift work in a couple of years, and it couldn't have come at a better time to enable me to focus more on the family – my first ministry. Other than delivering policy and legislative changes from Scotland Yard, I saw this role as on the job training for my colleagues to informally assist them around race and equality issues. I also took this role to the community who had negative perceptions of the police, especially young people, by speaking to students from local schools and colleges who wanted to know what it was like to be a black officer in the Met.

Christmas came and my parents invited us all round for a Christmas dinner. They lived in Islington, just up the road from where Gretl's sister lived. At the Christmas dinner, Gretl reiterated that she was not coming back. Gerad and Leah were both very distressed; I said to Gretl, 'Let's talk about this, because this is hurting all of us.'

New Year came. I knew that for the children's sake, I couldn't leave things as they were. By this time, they'd been without their mum for a couple of months, and Gerad was really beginning to miss her. He did see her from time to time – she was at his aunt's house and it wasn't that far away – but that's not the same as having Mum at home when you get in from school. 'Mum will come home, trust me,' I'd say to reassure him. I needed to work this out with Gretl. Children are resilient, but they need their mothers. I wanted our children to realize that Mum and Dad might have their problems, but they'll always work things out, based on a foundation of love.

My birthday was coming up, and I asked Gretl to meet me and have a conversation. She was working in the city of London and the Barbican Centre was easy for both of us to get to, so we agreed to meet there for coffee. After we'd had our coffees, I went to the Gents. When I came back, there was a note on our table.

'I'm going to the toilet,' Gretl announced, and headed off in search of the Ladies. I opened up the note. It said, 'I'm not coming back to this marriage unless God is in it.'

'I've read the note,' I said when Gretl returned. 'I thought God was in our relationship.'

'Not any more,' Gretl said. 'You're just too much into your own ambitions. You need to understand the importance of your faith and your family.'

'Well, have you got an idea of how we're going to do this?' I asked.

'There's a church that meets in Islington just up the road from where I am. I'd like you to come along.'

'Okay,' I said.

That Sunday, I went to Islington Green School where the London Church of Christ (LCC) held its services. I liked the energy I encountered in the church; it was full of young people and very vibrant, with a strong emphasis on the Bible, on discipleship and on street evangelism. At the same time, however, I noticed a few things that bothered me a bit. For starters, they seemed to highlight people who did well in their street evangelism work, but then made the others feel guilty for not doing so well. They'd divided London into points of the compass: the North, South, West and East Zones. The leaders would say, 'The West Zone brought in more souls this week than the East Zone did.' I'd like to think that was to motivate people to greater effort, but to me it seemed more designed to create guilt and a sense of failure. At times it felt as though you were seen to be lacking in faith if you didn't get that many people into the church through street evangelism. We lived in Walthamstow at the time and so attended East Zone meetings.

The church membership was mostly very young with a lot of members either at university or just starting their careers. In contrast, Gretl and I were well into our thirties. I made some observations, but I liked Tim and Chevy, the pastors heading up the East Zone. Tim was both a qualified vet and now a pastor. I think he wanted to give me special treatment as his police sergeant who was part of his zone. He took on the role of mentoring me through Bible study, and it worked, since we got on well and Tim lived in Woodford, just down the road from us. He was still doing a certain number of vet calls, and so we would go to farms in Essex and see the farmers; he would tend to their livestock and then we'd go horse riding. He taught me how to ride a horse; I returned the favour by arranging to take him on a drive-around so that he could experience police work. Unfortunately, a murder happened on the evening of the planned drive-around, and so we had to shelve it while I went off to investigate.

This combination of discipleship and horse riding classes went on for a few months. During that time, there was a great emphasis on being born again and baptized by immersion, and also on tithing. Having observed the changes in me, Gretl came back home with Myles, and we both got into the Word; we were 'fired up', as the LCC folks used to say. Tim's method of mentoring me was to treat me as an equal. He never talked down to me, but he broke everything down. I remember him expounding on a scripture in Timothy that talks about the word of God being 'God-breathed'. I'd heard and read it before, but it never had the same impact as when Tim explained it to me. I remember saying afterwards, 'There's no excuse not to be born again.'

Gretl and I found a kindred spirit in another couple we met in the church, Rob and Donna Neil. They attended the West

Zone, and were baptized the same weekend in February 1994. We started to compare notes; as we did so, we began to notice how controlling the church could be. Although Gretl and I were treated quite well, I noticed certain things happening to other members that left me feeling uncomfortable. I didn't question my faith as a result of that; instead Rob and I decided to investigate the LCC a bit more. We learned that it had Mormon roots, and that raised some concerns for us.

Meanwhile, the pastor in charge of the West Zone twigged that two of his flock were fraternizing with people from the East Zone. Tim came to me one day and asked, 'Have you been speaking to someone in the West Zone?' I said, 'Yeah, we met at the central church.'

That was the first time I noticed the church's controlling tendencies directed at me. Then came 12 February – Gretl's birthday. Gretl had been quite busy at work and I was involved in loads of operational work, so we had decided to forgo having a big celebration and to have a quiet evening in instead. All of a sudden – and totally unannounced – Tim and Chevy turned up with the rest of the church team. They'd found babysitters for us and bought us tickets to see the C. S. Lewis film *Shadowlands*.

Inside, I was thinking, '*I'll* tell you if I want to go and see a movie, thank you very much', but I played along, and we went. It was a good film, but we were more concerned about why they were doing this. Were they trying to control us? I appreciated the offer, but I didn't like the way they'd gone about it without consulting us first. Even though they meant well, that was the beginning of the end of our time at the LCC. We started to challenge the pastors on everything. I didn't want to at first, but something in my spirit told me I needed to. They didn't take it very well when I mentioned the research I'd been doing. 'Why are you doing that?' they asked. 'Don't get involved in anything that doesn't concern you.' They quoted another scripture from

Timothy at me, but tried to imply that it meant I should shut up and know my place. 'If that's your attitude,' I thought, 'it's best that we leave.'

And so we left. It took a long time for us to extricate ourselves spiritually because we'd forged a strong connection with the church – especially Gretl. She had discovered the church and brought me into it, so she was the hardest hit when we left. We started going to All Souls Langham Place with Rob and Donna, who had also jumped ship with us, and we've been maintaining our strong family fellowship with them ever since.

There is one thing we all have to acknowledge in life: the fact that 'Change is a constant' and the Met is no exception. Without any reasonable notice, Scotland Yard initiated another form of sector policing to ensure borough officers become more citizen-focused, through assigned sector officers working consistently at a local level. After only a few months as the divisional trainer, I was asked to be a sergeant in charge of the Hackney Central Sector officers, playing to my strengths in community policing. Through the gathering of reliable community intelligence, I was quickly tasking my sector constables to carry out proactive operations on organized local criminals, with the intention of making safer communities – especially those gripped by fear of the local drug dealers, robbers and burglars.

Little did I know that, after a great start, everything would come to a grinding halt while I was carrying out some undercover work. On this particular afternoon, I'd finished athletics training and gone to rejoin the officers on a surveillance operation I was coordinating. There was a crack house in Seven Sisters near Manor House, and we'd taken up surveillance in a nearby church. It was a big church and we were observing from the vicar's office – which, to me, felt quite poetic: a Christian copper in a church, watching a crack house.

Another officer and I noticed the main dealer coming out of the crack house with a big bag. We assessed from his previous transactions that it contained either drugs or money, or maybe even both. We decided to leave the observation point with a colleague manning it, to go and stop him. It was a judgement call; we'd called for backup, but everyone was busy. And we were using the old radio system which didn't have an emergency button, so we couldn't just cut in and ask for assistance. As soon as we identified ourselves as police officers, the dealer started to shout and scream about police harassment. Before long, we were surrounded by a menacing crowd, as I was telling the suspect that he was under arrest on suspicion of supplying drugs.

The dealer broke free from my grip and ran across Seven Sisters Road, where he ran into a police car from another division. He hit the car, swivelled round and continued running into the estate. Having just come from training, I felt up for the challenge, and so I ran after him. He was young and quite fit, but I was closing in fast. By now we were in the estate, running down a corridor in one of the blocks. I grabbed hold of him just as he was going through a doorway. He swung the door back; my ankle got caught between the door and the doorframe. I heard a loud crack that sounded like a gunshot, and I dropped like a stone. My ankle had shattered, and I was in agony. The crack was so loud, it echoed across the corridor. I could hear the officer behind me saying on his radio, 'Urgent assistance, officer down. Officer down'. He ran up to me. 'Are you all right?' he asked. 'Have you been shot?'

'No,' I replied. 'I've just messed up my ankle on the door. Go after him once back up arrives.'

The suspect was eventually apprehended, but he'd disposed of the bag's contents by the time we caught him. I went to St Bartholomew's Hospital that night and was told that there was no bone injury, but I knew that couldn't be right; I'd heard the crack. The other officer had heard it too. And I'd been training for many years, so I knew when something was not right. I was immediately signed off as sick, and that gave me a great deal of time to reflect on this devastating experience. Yet at the same time, somehow, I felt it was meant to be, because what it did was slow me down.

A couple of weeks passed, and the swelling showed no signs of going down. I went back to Bart's, and again they said, 'We've checked the x-rays; there's nothing wrong'. By this time I was back at work, but on light duties because I could hardly walk. Fortunately for me, I was not on response team, and I could still run the Hackney Central Sector office with my injured leg.

I did have to ask, why had God slowed me down? 'God, I know you haven't done this just for the sake of it,' I said. 'You're testing me.' The Bible verse that kept coming to my mind was Job 23:10: 'But he knows the way that I take; when he has tested me, I will come forth as gold.' I was being tested. I just knew it. But for what? And after a few days, a light bulb came on: *The Black Police Association!* This was why God wanted me to join the police service: to be part of changing the organization via the BPA!

I might have just been being fanciful, but that moment was when everything crystallized for me. I'd been in the job 11 years up to this point, and everything fell into place as to why I had joined and why the Lord wanted me to stop and reflect. And the only way to do that was for me to break my ankle!

Spiritually, I never had one of those dramatic 'Damascus road' conversion experiences. The London Church of Christ people had been very big on baptism, and Gretl had got baptized there. I knew I'd given my life to Christ, but I did wonder where the purpose was in all this. Shortly after the ankle injury, I was at the Bloomsbury Baptist Church, having received an invitation to hear a sermon from the American civil rights leader Jesse

Jackson. He was there to commemorate Martin Luther King's preaching there 30 years previously in 1964. Jesse Jackson was preaching on chapter 12 of Paul's Epistle to the Romans, and the second verse, about being transformed by the renewing of your mind, really hit me. Suddenly that sense of purpose I'd been struggling to find became clear and obvious. That really was my epiphany experience: on the pews of Bloomsbury Baptist Church, with the great Jesse Jackson delivering the message. If there was ever a time to get the message, I couldn't think of a better time and place.

That first half of 1994 brought about a paradigm shift in my thinking. I spent two weeks at home convalescing after the injury. It sounds like a short time, but it was enough for my purpose in the Met to become clear to me. It was great doing all the athletics and the sporting activities, but it was now time to focus more on central strategic issues. At the same time, I was a born again Christian and working out where I was as an individual. I became more purposeful in what I was trying to do, realizing that I couldn't just do it through my primary role as a sergeant; it had to be a wider process of enhancement and self-empowerment. I had to rethink my long-term career strategy anyway, as the Met had introduced a moratorium that effectively halted my prospects for promotion. Hackney was a crucible. If you're working there, you have to come out as gold; you have to show excellence. And so I realized I had to see my time there as a time to get close to my Maker and get in line with what he sent me out to do as a police officer. I was absorbing stuff like a sponge: reading the Bible, learning about a purpose-driven life through Myles Munroe publications, and generally ensuring that I stuck to what I had to do and didn't get derailed.

Six months later, I had an MRI scan. I had to go private in the end; the scan revealed that I'd lost about an inch and a half of tibia at the base of my ankle and all the bone fragments were still floating around in the joint. I had to have keyhole surgery to remove it all. That was when I knew I was halted in my tracks for a reason, because then I could stop being into so many different things and focus on my family, my faith, and on what God wanted me to do in the Met through the BPA. I took on more responsibilities in the BPA and ended up becoming its treasurer. That was my first official BPA role – that and being part of the planning team for the launch on 26 September 1994.

When we officially informed the Commissioner Sir Paul Condon and his management board of our constitution, they didn't immediately support us – which, I believe, gave the Federation a certain amount of mileage to come criticizing us even more. I suppose they were trying to create the fear factor so we would dissipate and scatter. Instead, we became even more resolute. We knew why we were doing this. It wasn't to be self-serving, but to speak on behalf of the black community. For me, it was a no-brainer that we had to stick to our principles.

There were a lot of challenges leading up to the BPA launch, as I have said before. We had chosen our post holders, and we had a chair, a deputy chair and a general secretary. Mike Fuller was the initial interim chair; as September approached, he stepped back, and Ron Hope took over. I took on the role as treasurer. It wasn't glamorous; in fact, no one else wanted to do it, but I thought I should step up and show willing, and at the same time learn as much as I could about being a change agent: hone my leadership skills and learn how to bring people with me in what I wanted to do for the greater good.

We got more and more criticism about the BPA at work. But I was confident in what I was doing so I was able to fend that off and say that if things were so perfect, we wouldn't have formed in the first place. There wouldn't have been any need for a BPA if there wasn't a hostile environment in the Met, in particular for ethnic minority personnel.

When we finally had our launch, it was phenomenal. I remember being one of the officers who received our guests in the reception at New Scotland Yard. You could see the white officers thinking, 'Why are all these people here?' Many people of note came: people such as Sir Herman Ouseley, the chair of the Commission for Racial Equality (CRE). There were people of prominence from all walks of life, like High Commissioners from Africa and the Caribbean, who contributed to creating a positive atmosphere. It wasn't a big media event, but nevertheless it was a historic one.

It was a time of reflection for us as well. We'd occupied those same seats in the conference room in 1990 when the Bristol Seminars were announced. Little did we know then that we would be doing this four years later.

I remember the commissioner appearing at the launch and saying, 'I could sit on the fence, but it's an uncomfortable place to be. So I've got to be for you or against you – and I'm for you.' We accepted it, but it felt as if he'd been forced into that position. But again, we weren't discouraged by that. A bit disappointed maybe, but we weren't expecting everyone to be in full support of what we were doing. Whenever you try to change an organization from within, you will encounter opposition. This was echoed by our chair, Ron Hope, who was a chief inspector in Lambeth. He was able to give a strong visionary speech that mobilized and inspired us. We left with a spring in our step, with our families and friends who shared our trust in Ron. And while this was going on, the Stephen Lawrence investigation was exposing more ugly truths about racism within the police.

Another high-profile murder case was creating a buzz on the other side of the Atlantic at this time. I watched the O. J. Simpson trial every day. Seeing the hostility it created in American life and that sense of trial by media was quite telling. But I was impressed by Johnnie Cochran and how he defended OJ. It was real theatre. While that trial was coming to its conclusion, we had a meeting with Peter Herbert, chair of the Society of Black Lawyers, Lee Jasper, director of the 1990 Trust, and Lloyd LaRose Jones of the Association for Black Probation Officers. They were planning to host a series of conferences called Race for Justice, with Johnnie Cochran as keynote speaker. I thought, 'Wow – that guy I've been watching on TV is going to be your keynote speaker? If he succeeds and OJ is acquitted, there's no way he's going to come to little old London.'

Dave Michael was elected to succeed Ron Hope as BPA chair in October 1995. He was a detective inspector based in Lime-house, Tower Hamlets. We used to talk to each other regularly, and occasionally take time out over lunch to encourage each other. We needed to do that because we were getting so much heat in our respective divisions, both of us being seen as trou-blemakers by others in the station. I'd been perceived as one from the get-go at Hendon, so it was nothing new to me. But others reacted differently. As I have said, we lost some people because of the pressure that was being placed on them. Those times of fellowship that Dave and I had together helped us both cope with all that was being thrown at us in east London.

I saw this not just as a job above my primary role; I saw it as God's purpose in my life. It was kingdom work; it was advanc-ing a kingdom of fairness, justice and equality and setting back the strongholds of inequalities and injustices, sending a light into the darkness of those corridors that normally wouldn't see the light. There were still areas of the organization we didn't know about, such as the Special Demonstrations Squad (SDS): an undercover unit that's part of Special Branch, and whose function is to infiltrate protest groups. We discovered that the SDS had been investigating Stephen Lawrence's family. I'm sure they must have been investigating us at some stage. We didn't know anything about the SDS until it was exposed decades later.

Dave Michael wanted to make some real changes. During the Race for Justice conference at the Commonwealth Institute, Dave declared at the press conference that racism was endemic in the police service. This had never been said so openly before, and it caused a media storm. And as we were there with him, the media pounced on us. It was such an unexpected experience, and it was burden-removing that we were saying it as it is: we weren't just acquiescing; we were standing up. And we created our own platform in which to do that. We had a foreword from the MP Bernie Grant. Johnnie Cochran came over from the USA to speak; other guests included the barrister Michael Mansfield QC.

The Race for Justice conference was our coming out party. It was us saying, 'We're here. We're a force to be reckoned with; a force for good.' I saw the BPA as a force to focus on wider injustices in society, and that did not exclude the police. It was clear to me that I could not in any way step back from that. We felt mobilized and galvanized, and we knew that we were going to get a lot of pushback.

Dave's statement did not go down well with the Federation. He was summoned to a meeting with a member of the management board, to explain how he could make such a speech without notes. He told the senior manager that he could do so because he was speaking from his lived experience. I will always admire him for stepping up in that way. It gave us a level of prominence; it made people aware that we were prepared to tell it as it is – and, if need be, to name and shame.

We could see the effects of our efforts starting to bear fruit. Through our constitution, we were rewriting the rulebook on how to deal with diverse personnel, and how they can speak up for themselves and add value to an organization. One of our objectives was to assist with recruiting into the Met. We knew we had a role to play in attracting people to the organization.

People admired us for that, and they did join the organization because they saw members of the BPA being clear on what we were there to do as role models.

The Bristol reunions continued. At the 1996 one, we took a collection for the Lawrence campaign, who had begun a private prosecution against the suspects in Stephen's murder. We promptly handed over the spontaneous collection to the Lawrences to assist with the prosecution (which sadly failed). We were getting some real prominence and rubbing shoulders with some quite significant people – including Mike Mansfield, whom we'd got to know through the Race for Justice conference, and who was now representing the Lawrences. We were also getting requests from minority ethnic officers in other countries, such as Denmark, Norway and Holland, because of the inequalities and injustices they were experiencing.

We were also getting national attention, as well as international, from black police officers elsewhere in the UK, who were interested in what we were doing. Initially, this interest came from three ex-Met officers – Ray Campbell, Pat Harris and Ludlow Johnson – who had transferred to Northampton in the 1980s. With our support from the Met, they subsequently launched a BPA there in 1995. With that, a wider network of officers who identified as black began to grow, and another BPA was launched in Bedfordshire some months later, under the leadership of Ravi Chand. I really respected these officers for standing up for equality and justice in relative isolation, in comparison with those of us in London. We were in much larger numbers, experiencing greater confidence in a critical mass of black officers and civil staff in the Met BPA movement.

Our support network gave assistance to black officers and police staff who had been the victims of inappropriate supervision. This took on many forms: including a lack of proper appraisals, being discouraged from taking promotion, and a disproportionate number of personnel being subjected to disciplinary measures. A few of them were strong enough to take out legal proceedings – employment tribunals or civil actions – and we were supporting them. Those of us who were giving support to others often had to do it in our free time. Depending on how good your relationship with your line manager was, if someone needed help during your working hours, you could ask your boss for some time off to go and tend to them. I was fortunate back then in that I was more or less my own boss and not subject to the goodwill of a supervisor or the lack of it. My inspector did give me a lot of responsibility, as the Hackney Central Sector sergeant, but he was very positive and let me have the time I needed to do support work. After a while, as the Met BPA negotiated some facility time, there were set times when a member of the support network could go and offer help to whoever needed it. We were getting busier and busier because successful cases attracted more people, and our paid membership grew exponentially.

The number of cases coming our way was overwhelming. One that really hit us happened in Manchester in 1995, when two black Met officers went undercover on a drug deal. Their identities were compromised, and they had to defend themselves from the perpetrators, who had guns. The officers escaped, but in the process, both were shot. We received a call that they were in a hospital only a stone's throw from the scene of the shooting, and they were not being protected – even though the perpetrators could easily go to the hospital and finish the job. I knew the officers; one was based in Tower Hamlets, and the other was based in Hackney with me. Members of our executive had to go up there and support them, and speak to the Manchester senior officers to ensure the officers and their families were adequately protected. Again, we got a reputation for being troublemakers and were accused of over-reacting, but it was the right thing to do. We were rewriting the rule books to support black personnel who were victims of the hostile environment in the police service.

Meanwhile, a retired American air force officer called Jerome Mack and his wife Francesca convinced the Home Office to support them in running national diversity courses for police officers. The courses took place in Turvey, and so the graduates were commonly known as Turvey graduates. I was invited to share my experience as a black officer. Similarly, I made contributions to the national police training centres in different parts of the country, including Harrogate and Bramshill, where the strategic command course was being taught. As a number of contributors did, I would speak very plainly about the plight of black people in the Police Service and how that was similar to the treatment of black people in society, reinforcing perceptions that the police were against them and not for them. Certain communities have a lack of trust and confidence in the police because they believe they are over-policed and under-protected. This was a massive eye-opener for a lot of the officers who attended; they had never heard this from a black officer before. It was a wake-up call. But it was questionable whether they would take action in their respective force areas or would be allowed to do so.

Ron Hope went to work at Turvey, and I worked with him to form a network of black officers we subsequently called the National Communication Network. It was our way of spreading infectious optimism and maintaining the momentum from our launch of the Met BPA, followed by those in Northants and Bedfordshire. I chaired the inaugural meeting in Bramshill, the police college for senior leaders, of a dynamic group of black officers across the country who were movers and shakers in the race equality agenda, and looking at setting up a BPA or its equivalent in their force area. It was clear to me at the time this group would be the foundation for a national body, and I ensured we met up regularly to make it happen.

8

'Don't show us in a bad light'

Even though the Lawrence family's private prosecution hadn't been successful, they had garnered much support – especially after Nelson Mandela met them and took a personal interest in the case. When the Labour Party came to power in May 1997, one of their first announcements was that there would be an inquiry into Stephen's death.

Sir William Macpherson (now Lord Macpherson) was assigned to preside over the inquiry. One of the members of the panel set up to support him was Dr Richard Stone. I knew Richard well; he was a prominent GP who had given up his medical practice to become a fighter for equality and justice and to assist deprived communities. He had a family fund that helped many different charities, including the Notting Hill Carnival – which, like him, was based in west London. He helped a lot of people who weren't getting the assistance they needed through the statutory organizations.

I've always found different faiths' places of worship fascinating. I had visited mosques and temples, but so far, I hadn't been to a synagogue. I arranged with Richard to have a tour of one near Marble Arch. As he was showing me the Torah, the scrolls and different areas of the synagogue, Richard mentioned that he'd been approached to be on the Lawrence inquiry panel, and asked whether I thought he should accept the invitation. I thought it was quite surreal, him asking me this in a synagogue, of all places. But when would I have another opportunity to encourage someone to be on the panel for a national inquiry?

'You'll be perfect for it,' I said. 'You never go into things with preconceived ideas. You always go with a fresh perspective.'

By this time, I was still based in Hackney, in charge of the central sector community team. The moratorium on promotions was about to be lifted, so I began my preparations for the new format national inspector's exam with a great deal of confidence in my abilities and knowing I would be a strong candidate, equipped with nine years' experience as a sergeant. I found it poignant that my progress in passing the exam with flying colours was being made against the backdrop of the announcement of the Macpherson Inquiry.

The first phase of the Inquiry was about the investigation: what were the issues leading up to that incident and the subsequent investigation, and why were no suspects charged? They had been arrested, some of them repeatedly, but they were in and out before you knew it. The racism, corruption and incompetence of the investigation team were key issues that were coming out.

The second phase focused on the implications for policing and wider organizations and the public. This was where the BPA was asked to contribute. Three of us wrote up a submission to present to the Inquiry: myself, Paul Wilson and Bevan Powell. Paul was also an inspector based in south London and was chair of the BPA. Bevan was an executive member of the BPA and a higher executive officer in the Met.

On the strength of our written evidence, we were asked to give public evidence. You could sense the growing anxiety among our white work colleagues in the lead-up to our appearance at the inquiry. This was going to shine a light on the organization again, but this time it was going to be really profound because we were saying publicly that the police service was institutionally racist. Just as with the Bristol Seminars years before, people would ask us, 'What are you going to say?' – followed by 'Don't show us in a bad light.' They didn't always say it that explicitly, but they hinted at it very strongly. None of that fazed us; these things had to be said. At the same time, we had to reflect clearly how we were going to say things. Whatever we said, it had to be evidence-based and not subjective: we were not going to hold back from speaking truth to power.

The inquiry was held at Hannibal House, a multi-storey building that sits on top of the Elephant and Castle shopping centre in south London. I remember how it felt when Paul, Bevan and I went there to give evidence in the inquiry. A few months earlier, it had been the scene of a wave of hostility when the suspects were required to give evidence. You could still sense that hostility in the atmosphere when we went, even though the crowds of protesters that had been there when the suspects gave evidence were not there this time.

When we sat in front of the panel to speak, it was like Bristol all over again. We let everything out: all the casual racist comments we regularly experienced like the N-words and monkey noises we had to put up with on the communication radio system, in the canteen or on the beat, and all the low- and high-level racism that had become part and parcel of my working life since I joined the organization 15 years earlier. We told the panel that things shouldn't be the way they were – that the culture in the organization was racially biased. It wasn't just racist individuals: there were systemic failures that lead to institutional racism. We knew, as we gave our evidence, that we had broken certain taboos within the organization. You don't breach that kind of camaraderie or push back on misplaced loyalties and then walk away unscathed.

There were some senior officers present, sitting behind us. We could hear them tutting and sighing as we spoke. But we could also see the panel in front of us absorbing everything we were saying. The looks on their faces said what they were thinking:

'It's about time someone told it as it is.' Those 90 minutes went by in a flash. When we finished giving our evidence, I said, 'I want to acknowledge the strength of character and the resolve of the Lawrence family for what they've done. I would like you to pass that onto them.'

'You can say it to them yourself,' Lord Macpherson said. 'They're right behind you.'

Both Doreen and Neville were very appreciative of what we said. They knew we had spoken up at the risk of our own careers and personal lives, and that forged an ongoing relationship with them. This meant the Met BPA had the opportunity to volunteer at the annual Stephen Lawrence memorial services, and to attend the launch of the Stephen Lawrence Charitable Trust building in southeast London. It also led to Neville Lawrence accepting the position of patron to the BPA charitable trust work, which is now known as Voyage Youth.

Ian Johnston, the assistant commissioner, was heavily grilled by the panel as the Met's representative regarding its internal and external systemic failures, not just in the Lawrence investigation but in the organization as a whole. I know there was a great deal of pressure on him as the public face of the Met on those issues. In fact, the uniform appeared to weigh heavily on him as he appeared to age from a smiling fresh-faced effervescent personality to a regularly frowning, thoughtful and more reserved person.

Our Met BPA submission was there to influence the report recommendations, and resulted in its conclusion that 'Institutional racism permeates the Metropolitan Police Service. This issue above all others is central to the attitudes, values and beliefs, which lead officers to act, albeit unconsciously and for the most part unintentionally, and treat others differently solely because of their ethnicity or culture.' Referring to our contribution, the report stated: 'The oral evidence of the three representatives of the MPS Black Police Association was illuminating. We believe that it is essential that the views of these officers should be closely heeded and respected.'

If our views were heeded, it was done grudgingly by many in the Met, but nobody questioned the integrity and relevance of our evidence.

With the Macpherson Report in the offing, it was clear that the BPA needed to have a national voice. By this time, Paul Wilson was chair of the London BPA and I reported to him. I said to him, 'Paul, with the recommendations of the Macpherson Inquiry, the National Communication Network (NCN) is going to be prominent, mainly because it channels the desires of black personnel across the country.' I also emphasized 'You really need to come to the next NCN meeting.' Having attended all of the regular meetings following the inaugural one I set up at Bramshill a couple of years earlier, I had observed first-hand the critical mass of black personnel developing an unquenchable thirst for a national voice. Despite my efforts to convince him of how important it was, however, Paul didn't see the need to attend the next meeting.

One of the other officers who had immediately jumped on board from the first NCN meeting was Dave McFarlane, a fellow member of the Met BPA. He was very good at drawing people into the call for action, and was spending a lot of time mobilizing people nationally. I didn't realize how much influence Dave had in the Home Office, but he had been having meetings with senior officials, especially after the Home Secretary Jack Straw attended the Met BPA AGM in October 1998, a few months after we had given evidence at the Macpherson Inquiry.

'We need to have a national organization,' Dave said to me.

'We've got a critical mass of people behind us,' I replied. 'There are now BPAs in Northamptonshire and Bedfordshire, and interested individuals in Nottingham and Manchester. Let's go for it.'

Acting as a go-between, Dave reported that the Home Office was also eager that black personnel had a national voice in time for the Macpherson Report, due to be published in a matter of months, which meant the NCN meeting in November 1998 was going to vote on a national executive. It was clear to me that the tide was irreversibly changing, and we had to take the opportunity to build our national platform. If the national executive was not formed in time for the Macpherson Report publication in February 1999, then it would not be in a position to own the recommendations that would have a seismic change on policing nationally.

I said to Bevan Powell, 'You've been coming to these meetings with me; what should we do?'

'We need to attend the meeting and fully assess how we can influence events,' Bevan said.

Someone who'd started to build prominence leading up to this meeting was an officer called Ali Dizaei. Ali was a chief inspector in Thames Valley. He was a very prominent officer; he had recently completed a PhD on racism and policing, and he was a qualified barrister. Consequently, I had heard of him being a mover and shaker in his constabulary area, not shying away from confronting the issues based on his research. Ali had never been to an NCN meeting before, but he came to this one and it seemed as if he knew what was going to happen. Lo and behold, when the election came up, Ali Dizaei was the only candidate for national chair. This guy who had just appeared from out of nowhere was about to be our national chair, in some form of coronation. Something in me said, 'This isn't right. You need to step up.'

Bevan echoed my thoughts. 'You've got to throw your hat in the ring, Lee,' he said.

'But I'm only the treasurer of the London BPA,' I said. 'How can I put myself forward just like that, without the Met BPA executive's backing?'

Things were going at a hundred miles per hour and I was trying to think. 'Lord', I prayed, 'what do you want me to do?'

The presiding officer hosting the meeting from the front then interrupted my prayer. 'Who else is putting themselves forward?'

Heart pounding, I raised my hand. 'I am,' I said.

About fifty people voted, drawn from police services across the country. It was such a surreal moment when it was announced that I'd been elected as the first chair of the National Black Police Association. I thought, 'What have I taken on!' This was immediately offset by the election of a dynamic team that included Ali as my deputy chair and Bevan as a member of the executive

I phoned Paul Wilson on the way back, and said, 'This thing just went up to another level. I couldn't allow Ali to waltz in and become our national chair.' Paul seemed quite philosophical about it, but when I met him at an executive meeting a day or so later, he was extremely abrupt towards me in front of the executive. As the current Met BPA chair at a very dynamic time, it was unacceptable and unnecessary.

I said, 'Paul, I told you to come to the meeting.'

'You shouldn't have done it,' Paul said. 'You should have walked away.'

'And then what?' I said. 'I didn't have any intention of doing it, but I had to step up for the greater good, especially since I set up the NCN in the first place, and that led to the formation of the national executive.'

I knew that things would never be the same between Paul and me after that, and they weren't. It was a disappointment, but I wouldn't allow myself to be discouraged from carrying out my purpose. Paul and I had been at training school together; we were promoted to sergeant and inspector about the same time; we worked on the Bristol Seminar report together; and we were founder members of the BPA, who had given evidence together at the Macpherson Inquiry. We had gone through many challenges together, and he was unwilling to give me the benefit of the doubt, which was astonishing. But that was his decision; there was nothing I could do about it.

I was very thankful to have Bevan with me at this time, especially since he was a fellow Christian and a very objective person. The fact that he had spurred me on to run for the chair position was, for me, an endorsement. Bevan became a very active and long-standing member of the National BPA.

With my twin roles as chair of the National BPA and treasurer of the London one, I decided that I needed to have more of a strategic role than just being a response team inspector in Enfield. And so, in November 1998, I applied for a role at Hendon as an intake manager, training and supervising new recruits. I wouldn't be on shift work, so I would be a lot more accessible, working more at the centre of things. I got the job and started in the role in January 1999.

My aim was just to be National BPA chair for a year in order to get the foundations of our constitution right, all ready for the official launch in November 1999, which was to be held at the International Conference Centre in Birmingham. There was a lot to do in a short space of time. I still felt hurt by Paul's response. I couldn't see why he was so hostile to me, and it wasn't getting any better. The fall-out had wider implications, as our families used to meet up at social events, invariably around the BPA network. Leadership can be a lonely place.

When the Macpherson Report was published in February 1999, the Met BPA took ownership of the 70 recommendations to ensure it had a pivotal role in the roll-out, working closely with the commissioner's lead officers Denis O'Connor (assistant commissioner), John Grieve (deputy assistant commissioner) and Bill Griffiths (deputy assistant commissioner). As a member of the executive team, I also played a pivotal role in working with all three, who were legends in the Met. They welcomed this, especially because I had my other role as chair of the National BPA, which gave me added influence. In particular, it was great to be working with John again, after a lapse of ten years, now in his new role as director of the Race and Crime Task Force, still displaying his consistent form of transformational leadership – a fellow maverick.

At the same time, people contacted me in a personal capacity, and continuously encouraged me and the work I was doing. Some would add they were praying for me, and passed on scripture verses. One in particular was of such relevance – Proverbs 22:29, 'Do you see someone skilled in their work? They will serve before kings.' Not only was I operating in the corridors of power at the Met level, but I was also operating at the ministerial level in the Home Office with Jack Straw MP and Paul Boateng MP, concerning the Macpherson recommendations, especially in setting targets for the recruitment, retention and progression of minority ethnic officers across the country. Again it confirmed to me the timeliness of having a national voice from a black perspective.

To assist in underpinning the targets, a great deal of behind the scenes work was carried out by me and other members of the National BPA, in concert with senior officials in the Home Office, where advisory reports made it clear that something different had to be done. Based on our advice, Jack Straw called an unprecedented national conference to be held in Southampton in May 1999, and he instructed every chief constable in the country to attend. It was another opportunity to speak truth to power, as I sat alongside Jack Straw and Paul Boateng on a panel, facing a wall of stern faces who presented a certain amount of deference in accepting my points as National BPA chair. Even though the bespoke targets set personally for each chief were ambitious in order to ensure the police service was representative of the community it served, the post-conference comments revealed a defeatist attitude: the chief constables seemed to believe that the targets were unattainable, and they did not see them as aspirational.

Being a panellist with Jack Straw and Paul Boateng was an unforgettable personal experience of shock and elation, but the follow-up work of my executive gave me the same amount of exhilaration, by having such a prominent role in changing policy. Nothing was more valuable than our position on the Stephen Lawrence Steering Group (SLSG). Chaired by Jack Straw in the presence of Doreen and Neville Lawrence, it monitored the relevant ministries rolling out the 70 recommendations from the Macpherson Inquiry across the country. I knew we would do that; I didn't know that we'd be doing it on a national stage, or with such a high profile. It was exciting interfacing with senior politicians, heads of departments and permanent secretaries. That again showed me that my national executive was a force for good, one to be reckoned with, and this sustained me spiritually, psychologically and physically.

It also gave me an insight on political access at ministerial and permanent secretary level as well as the realization that it could be a limited time, depending on the direction of the political head winds that could try and blow us out, if there were a change of ministers and a subsequent change in emphasis on race and equality issues. I also knew the smouldering giant of the national Police Federation and their allies would do whatever was necessary to undermine the BPA, nationally or locally. All of this reinforced my hyper-vigilance, the need to be on my guard 24/7, all year round. I had to remind myself that good times build confidence and bad times build character, not only for me but also for my national executive, and I had to engender both in my team in equal measure.

As the number of media and speaking engagements increased, I felt increasingly aware of something sinister going on. The unease I felt intensified as the launch of the Manchester BPA in May 1999 approached – so much so, I insisted that Gretl come to the launch with me. She didn't want to, but I begged her to. 'Please, just come with me,' I said to her. 'I don't know why, but I have a strong sense in my spirit that I need you to be there with me.' It was years later, when I found out that the Met was investigating me and other BPA members, that it reminded me, as if it needed to, of the importance of responding to my inner voice. Whenever I strayed from that inner direction, I suffered the consequences.

Before we knew it, Paul Boateng had moved on and Charles Clarke was in place to represent the Home Office and give the keynote speech at our inaugural AGM of the National BPA in November 1999. In the three-month period leading up to the event, Ali and I noticed that Clarke didn't mention diversity once in any of his speeches, and so we agreed that I would question him on it at our first formal meeting. Calling Charles Clarke out on his non-inclusivity showed people that we meant business. We could punch above our weight and we knew our issues. My purpose was clear; I was not going to feel inferior in any way. In fact, I felt emboldened – but I had to temper that boldness with wisdom.

We had some senior allies, but at the same time I could sense that we were acquiring some real enemies. I do believe this is what puts people off doing things that are radical; things capable of changing the norms and values and changing policy. A lot of people resented our work – not just within the Police Federation, not only locally in London, but nationally. They were always testing us, directly or indirectly, through other entities like the media.

One big test came after that Southampton conference at which we'd helped set the recruitment targets. All of a sudden, the Federation's national chair, Fred Broughton, was very keen to take my executive members and me to dinner with his top post holders. He took us to one of the most prestigious Indian restaurants in Victoria, one where all the parliamentarians frequently wined and dined.

We sat round an enormous table, and everyone was having good conversations. We could order whatever we wanted and drink whatever we wanted. It was quite friendly, but I'm always aware that there's no such thing as a free lunch. I knew I had to keep my wits about me. We had a very sumptuous five-course meal, and I thought, 'At last I've got something out of the Federation for all the subs I've paid all these years!'

At the end of the meal, Fred said, 'I would like to pass something by you.'

'Go ahead,' I said.

'We've got a new job recruiting campaign.'

'The Federation recruiting? Why would you want to do that?'

'I just feel that this is something that the Federation would do.'

He went on to explain that the Federation had enlisted the services of a marketing team, and they had come up with a concept for a series of posters playing on some stereotypical views of people of colour.

'It's a poster in two halves,' Fred explained. 'The top half is, let's say, an Asian woman who looks like she owns a grocery shop – a typical view of an Asian woman being a shop owner. When you reveal the bottom of the poster, it shows that she's actually a police officer in a station office.'

He then took one of the other posters out to show us. The top half was a black man in a BMW – the stereotypical view some people have of a black man in a flashy car. Where did he get it from? He must be up to no good. The 'reveal' was that he was actually a fast response driver in a high-performance police vehicle. Fred showed us a few more of these posters, then said, 'So, what do you think?'

'I'm still wondering why you want to get involved in this,' I said, 'but I've spotted a design flaw in these posters. If anyone goes up to one of them and tears off the bottom half, you're left with the stereotypical images of an Asian woman in a corner shop or a black man looking dodgy in a flashy car.'

I had to hold back my laughter because I could see that Fred was not happy. He must have paid this marketing team thousands of pounds to come up with this idea, and no one in his team had the cultural competence to tell him it wouldn't work. I looked at his executive post holders around the table. They were all white and only one of them was female. It suddenly dawned on me why we were being wined and dined in this fashion: it was to get us to approve these posters in response to our role in the recruitment, retention and progression targets.

'I still think it's worth your backing,' Fred said.

'I'm sorry,' I replied. 'Even if I wanted to back you I couldn't, because I don't make decisions unilaterally. Any backing for this would have to come from the National BPA executive.'

Instantly, the atmosphere changed. The smiles turned into frowns, and we felt an overwhelming urge to leave the premises. I was pleased that the rest of my team agreed with my assessment, but it didn't end there. We started to be called to the most senior meetings of the Association of Chief Police Officers (ACPO, which is now called the National Police Chief Council, NPCC). In those days, only chief constables or their nominees attended ACPO meetings. I was pleased that we'd got to the stage that we were being invited to them – and that it was through our own efforts, not through people pandering to us.

We'd been tested every step of the way, and because we worked closely with the Home Office, organizations like ACPO and the national Police Federation were reluctantly falling in line.

I was at an ACPO meeting on personnel and human resources, and Fred Broughton was there. At the end of the deliberations, the chair of the meeting asked if there was any other business. Without any prior warning, Fred stood up and gave his pitch for the recruitment posters. This time, I was the only BPA executive member present. I was so disappointed in him. I kept thinking, 'Why are you trying to ambush me like this?' It seemed as though a few other senior officers knew he was going to do it; as he was going through his presentation, they were nodding in approval – just as the Federation's national executive members had done a few days earlier in that Indian restaurant.

As Fred concluded his presentation, he said, 'I'm waiting for the National BPA's approval for this and we could roll this out nationally today.' I stared at Fred, almost in anger at his audacity. The scripture in which Jesus told his disciples to be 'as wise as a serpent and as innocent as a dove' came to my mind.

I immediately responded, 'As I said to Fred when he first produced these posters, even if I agreed with them, I cannot make a unilateral decision; it would have to go through the National BPA executive. He's aware of that. And I've already gone through the reasons why it won't work. If you tear off the bottom of each of those posters, all you are left with is the stereotypical image of those individuals.' As I spoke, I saw the expression on Fred's face. I knew that he now realized that his idea was dead in the water, and no one was going to endorse it if I had already set that tone.

Again, the atmosphere in the room changed – just as it had in that Indian restaurant the first time I'd rejected Fred's posters. You could see that there was some real animosity towards me and what I stood for. I'd already heard through the grapevine that people in ACPO had been asking who this 'self-appointed upstart' was, even though the BPA had a membership and it was those members who had voted me in.

Shortly after that test, I went with the rest of the executive team on a multi-city visit to the USA. We went from the East Coast through to the mid-West, touching down in Washington, New York and Chicago. It was quite an amazing opportunity to speak to our opposite numbers in the National Black Police Association over there, facilitated by the charismatic Ron Hampton. It was a ten-day whistle-stop tour, during which we had speaking engagements and sat in on some Senate committees. It was during a very hot July, which isn't the best time to go to the States! We went to a Senate committee in Chicago and heard Jesse Jackson speak. It was great to have a chance to speak to him afterwards. I shared with him the phenomenal impact his sermon had had on me, five years previously, at the Bloomsbury Baptist church in London, and how it made my God-given purpose so clear through my work in the BPA. I was so humbled by him knowing what we were doing in the UK, because he had been following the Stephen Lawrence case, especially after Nelson Mandela had intervened, which had set the wheels in motion for the inquiry. We also met another prominent civil rights leader, the Reverend Al Sharpton, who welcomed us as guests on his radio show.

Meeting such iconic people was a very inspiring experience, especially knowing their journeys and how many battles they'd fought in life. By the time we met Jesse Jackson, he'd spent about 40 years of his life fighting for human rights, and he still had all the strength he had had when he was marching next to Martin Luther King in the 1960s – you could feel it in his handshake!

The tour energized us and filled us with renewed confidence and a real sense of unity. I needed that boost; there was an almighty storm awaiting me back home.

***

I was six months into my new role as intake manager at Hendon. I had a very hard-working Blue Intake staff room team; one with a tendency to play as hard as they worked.

The rules are very strict regarding training staff having affairs or relationships with recruits that would bring us into disrepute. It's a big no-no, associated with clear sanctions. Unfortunately, it had happened quite a few times in the past with other staff teams before I got there. I was forever telling my team that we could not afford to have any sort of inappropriate relations with recruits. I also didn't want them telling recruits war stories about doing things on the job that were at odds with the way the manual had laid out those procedures correctly. I was adamant that we stick to the manual. Even as a recruit myself back in 1983, I'd observed that culture of bending the rules and not abiding by the manual – and that was still going on, 16 years later. It was almost like a form of internal radicalization by which recruits adopted the culture from the staff: the way they talked, the narratives they used, the swagger. It was like they were cloned in a very short space of time, a few weeks. Having observed that over the years, I decided that with my intake, I was going to ensure that we did things properly.

The first half of 1999 went like clockwork, by training hundreds of recruits in two cohorts who excelled academically and practically, maintaining the Blue Intake's reputation of success through positive team ethics under my leadership. Simultaneously I was successfully leading the National BPA role in owning the Macpherson Inquiry recommendations rollout across the country. Disappointingly, it started going wrong just before the passing out parade that July. It was going to be Sir Paul Condon's last passing out parade as commissioner. The dinner the night before the parade at a nearby hotel function room is an opportunity for the recruits to let their hair down – but not too much, as they have to get up at the crack of dawn to prepare for the big day. It was a tradition I didn't agree with, because of the obvious risks when large amounts of alcohol are consumed. Nevertheless, Gretl and I had a very nice time and left at a reasonable hour to go home, get some rest and return to Hendon. As I left, I said to my deputy, 'Please do what I said and get everyone back safe and sound.' As a longstanding member of Hendon staff, I accepted his reassurance that he would do so.

I went home, got some sleep and was back at work at 6 a.m. As I walked in, there was a strong smell of alcohol in the staff room. I saw my deputy and other members of the team. They all looked as though they hadn't slept.

'What's happened?' I asked my deputy.

'There was an incident last night,' he replied.

'What sort of incident?'

He explained that two recruits had been seeing each other. That in itself wasn't a problem; it is staff having relationships with recruits that's forbidden. However, these two had had an argument, and it was alleged that the male recruit had assaulted the female one. The night duty CID were called, and they did a search of the tower block the recruits lived in. There weren't that many female recruits, so the CID only had a few floors on one of the accommodation blocks to search. But when they did, they found a few male staff members in the rooms of some of the female recruits. Obviously, they had to take immediate action.

'Why wasn't I called?' I asked.

'There was nothing you could do,' came the reply.

'That's for me to decide,' I said. 'What's happening now?'

'That took all night. We haven't slept.'

They reeked of alcohol. 'Have you been drinking?' I asked.

Obviously, they hadn't stopped drinking at the appropriate time. Maybe that was why they'd felt emboldened to disobey my clear instructions. I knew then this was not going to end there. And it was the day before I was due to fly off to Canada for a holiday with Gretl and the children. I couldn't believe what was happening.

'The investigation can be done while I'm away,' I said. 'But we still need to do the passing out parade.'

We did the best we could, but the atmosphere was obviously marred by what had happened. We had to tell the commissioner about it beforehand, and that took all the joy out of the day. Before I left, I had a meeting with Mark Toland, the head of the recruit school. 'Leroy,' Mark said, 'when you come back from leave, your team will not be the same.'

My family and I had a great time in Canada. The children enjoyed themselves, and I got some quality time with them and Gretl. But I couldn't really enjoy the time away. Sometimes you can put things like this behind you, but every so often it would rear its head. As soon as our overnight homebound flight landed, a text message came through on my mobile phone: 'Contact Mark Toland.'

While we were in baggage reclaim retrieving our luggage, I called Mark. He said, 'Leroy, could you come in today?'

'We've literally just landed,' I said. 'But I'll drop the family and our bags off and come straight in.'

Gretl was not happy when I told her the news. 'What's happening?' she asked.

'It must be regarding the investigation and I need to go in,' I said.

I dropped Gretl and the children off at home. As I made my way in to work, I prayed: 'Lord, it's in your hands. Whatever I need to face, I'll face it full on.' When I arrived, Mark told me that most of my team had been transferred because they had breached the rules on fraternizing with recruits. Some had been moved back on to boroughs, some to different intake teams. Only one or two people remained.

Mark then told me that I'd been investigated in my absence, following a rumour that I was having an affair with a recruit called Francesca Azoba. I had been asked by the central recruiting branch to get involved in the making of a recruiting video aimed at people from minority groups, and Francesca had agreed to be filmed for it. We had spent some time in my section of the open plan office organizing the shoot with the production team, so everything we did was in full view of everyone else in the office. But that hadn't stopped people trying to turn it into something it wasn't.

According to the rumour, I had fathered a child with Francesca, and she'd had an abortion. In reality, she *had been* pregnant – by her fiancé – but unfortunately had suffered a miscarriage. This was another one of those times where I saw the closing of ranks at the expense of truth and justice, similar to the way they had closed ranks with my dad's civil case. My supervisors at Hendon realized the rumours were false when Francesca's fiancé came forward and said he was the father of her child and she had had a miscarriage. He wanted to speak to the officers who had concocted the rumour, but obviously they wouldn't let him. I felt those people should have been thrown out of the job, but they weren't.

The false story even made it into *The Sun*, but they reported it without mentioning names or any specific personal details; it just said 'A senior officer at Hendon was allegedly involved in a relationship with a recruit,' so it could have been anyone. I consulted lawyers to see if I had a case to sue *The Sun* or take action against the officers who had started the rumour, but unfortunately, I didn't have a strong enough case. I would see the officers from time to time and I'd think, 'You lot shouldn't be in the job, much less receive promotions, or make it to the end of your career.' I just didn't understand how such people could live with themselves and justify actions that were totally reprehensible.

My heart went out to Francesca. Using the terrible tragedy of losing a child to discredit her made me so angry, especially when I remembered when my mother had a miscarriage; I saw the pain in her face and the devastation it caused her. It hurt to think of this officer being devastated in the same way, and then being thrown into this cesspool of lies and deceit. But I couldn't see her because I was being investigated. In fact, I would see her from time to time through the Met BPA, as a valued member, but I never felt led to discuss it with her unless she raised it with me. She never did, and it was not until we were both retired in 2019, when I was writing this book, that I asked if she could give her side of this story to me. Even though twenty years had elapsed, it felt as if it were only yesterday, and I was thrown back into that extremely painful time for both of us, especially as she told me how she was pressured to implicate me for something I had not done. I was in total admiration of her strength of character and great resolve, in standing up to the pressure from senior officers, sticking to the truth despite the triple whammy of being a confused recruit, going through a personal tragedy, and being subject to a disgusting smear campaign by her teaching staff. They were making attempts to cover their own backs and point the finger of shame at me.

Even though I was completely exonerated, I knew rumours like that never really go away (and indeed they haven't; twenty years later, people are still spreading this on Twitter and Facebook). This shows the moral deficit the police culture can perpetuate, one that creates a hostile environment for many black officers. Many find it insufferable and leave in disproportionate numbers, as we have seen, especially in the first few years of their careers.

I knew that if someone could do this once, they could do it again, and so I decided to leave Hendon. I left without fanfare. With the launch of the National BPA coming up and all the work that would be involved in the roll-out of the recommendations Lord Macpherson had made in his Inquiry into Stephen Lawrence's murder, I had much bigger issues to contend with and I didn't want to expose my personal reputation, nor the office I held as national chair of the BPA movement, to any further risk. I went to see some senior officers at Scotland Yard and told them what had happened, and they suggested that I join the Positive Action Team: a recruiting team based in Westminster and tasked with rolling out the Lawrence recommendations on recruitment, retention and progression. It was a no-brainer; the Positive Action Team's remit fitted well with what I'd been doing as chair of the National BPA. Gretl was totally behind me on this move. I had to go to the BPA executive – both the national one and the London one – and here again, most people were fully supportive.

***

November was fast approaching, and the BPA national launch along with it. We ploughed all the advice and inspiration we'd gained from our summer tour of the USA into writing up the BPA constitution and strategic direction, ready to launch it at the International Conference Centre in Birmingham.

The conference was very full-on. So many media people wanted to speak to me; it was quite overwhelming. I never expected to be a media person, but I was thrust into that position and I couldn't step back from it. People were watching now. It wasn't just BPA members who were looking for me to speak up on their behalf; it was the wider public, in particular the black community.

As I'd planned, I stood down as National BPA chair at the launch conference. I was shocked when Paul Wilson (who had been so against me becoming the first chair) announced that he wanted to take over, even though he initially would not recognize my election and was very adversarial. Now there was this sudden change. I wasn't going to find out what was behind his change of heart since we hardly spoke to each other, despite my previous attempts to re-establish lines of communication to maintain unity. All I know is my faith had come to the rescue again, in strengthening my resolve to withstand the challenges to undermine me. I had made a success of my year as chair, and our movement had gone from strength to strength, with over ten BPAs, or their equivalents, having been launched in their respective constabulary areas. These were based on our newly formed constitution, fully recognized by the Home Secretary, because he saw us as a credible organization that added value in the modernization of policing across the country. I was more than happy to pass on the chair's baton.

At the back of my mind, I had a sense that whatever we did as the BPA, we had to be squeaky clean. In life, it's not so much what you do that gets you into trouble, as what you omit or forget to do. If you look at the lives of freedom fighters like Martin Luther King, their opponents tried to undermine them in terms of morality, their honesty, their finances, the way they conducted their lives and so forth. I knew the people who didn't like what the BPA was doing would try a similar tactic on me, to undermine the organization. Little did I know that as I was thinking this, they were actually drawing up a case against one of us.

Ali Dizaei and I worked well together, and as my deputy, I found him a formidable ally, both intellectually and physically. He was born in Iran and grew up in west London, and had some very rich friends. This gave some people the impression that he was somehow involved in unethical activity – nothing criminal, but there were suggestions that he was going into certain embassies (such as the Libyan embassy) without authority. And so, the Met had started to watch him as early as 1999.

We didn't know this at the time; another three years would pass before it all came out. At this time, I noticed my spiritual character was directing me just as much as my intellect and that unique mix kept me proactive. This led me to write a critical letter to Jack Straw, the Home Secretary, and Sir Paul Condon, the commissioner at the time, and to ACPO, outlining the concerns my executive and I had about individuals and organizations who could be party to a witch hunt and might join a conspiracy to undermine us. My revelations were based on white officers and police staff across the country informing us of these sinister individuals within their ranks. This letter turned out to be a strategic move, and it would be cited by others in future high profile race-based disciplinary cases, where our members were subject to higher levels of disciplinary action in comparison to their white counterparts.

In November 1999 we had the memorable launch of the National BPA in Birmingham, which put us on the map to reflect the views of black police personnel across the country, with a particular focus on the roll-out of the police-related recommendations from the Macpherson Inquiry. Having forged memorable professional relationships with members of the executive, I knew we had shared life-changing experiences that would influence our personal and professional lives.

Little did I know I would be soon having another life-changing experience...

I received a letter later that month from the Cabinet Office and then Buckingham Palace, informing me that I had been nominated for an MBE. If I accepted the award, I would receive it in January 2000. 'What a start to the millennium!' I thought and then my hyper-vigilance kicked in, convincing myself that it was a wind-up, an elaborate joke.

I quietly checked with senior officers, and was pleasantly surprised to discover that the nomination was genuine, made mainly with Jack Straw's approval for my contribution to policing. I didn't respond right away; I consulted with Gretl, the family and a few close friends before finally saying yes. When my parents gave me the green light, I had no hesitation in accepting it. It was just as much an award for them, for their sacrifices as part of the Windrush generation, which had given me opportunities to succeed against the obstacles that were thrown in my way. And so, it gave me the greatest privilege to dedicate my award to them in celebration of their journey 'from the boat to Buckingham Palace'.

Eventually I received my medal from the Queen at the award ceremony in the historic Throne Room of Buckingham Palace. It was a hot July day that year, and both Mum and Dad were in the audience along with Gretl, looking splendid. It was a great day, not only for the uniqueness of the occasion but because my father shared a few memorable words with me as we entered the Palace, where heads of state normally enter. Maybe that's why he chose that time and place to say, in his strong Jamaican accent, 'I suppose you did the right thing joining the police.' It took me totally by surprise, and momentarily I was rooted at the top of the stairs as I watched him walk towards Mum and Gretl, who were ahead of him in the queue for guests. I said, 'What did you say?' Without missing a stride, he extended his right arm with a thumbs up sign that took our relationship to another level of closeness, with the past barriers of disappointment totally erased in an instant.

I couldn't get that short exchange out of my mind as it constantly replayed itself, even as I received my medal from the Queen. I saw it as a vindication for responding to the call of policing and not following my journey of science, which (at the time of that professional transition) was my worst nightmare but turned out to be my biggest breakthrough. Looking back, it is incredible that I joined the Met, given how I felt about my experiences of policing in London, and particularly after what had happened to my dad.

It was such a long and exhilarating day, and it concluded with a post-ceremony service of thanksgiving and reception at St Margaret's Lothbury in the city of London, for family and friends, where I saw my parents more expressive and animated than I had ever seen them before. It brought such personal joy. Later, I would have to cling desperately to all the emotions and experiences of that day to assist me in coping with their unforeseen deaths through heart attacks: Mum in September 2001 and Dad in September 2002. They left a phenomenal legacy that I was determined to build on.

9

Westminster

One of the first things I realized when we started the BPA was that it was crucial for us to have charitable status. I drew up the Articles of Association in 1998 and got us registered with the Charity Commission. It was all new territory to me, but I felt led to do it, which was timely when we started to formulate plans for a community-based project in 2000. Here I added my personal commitment as the inspector in charge of the Westminster Partnership Unit, but also as Met BPA chair when I was elected in October that year.

Having worked on the Lawrence inquiry and knowing how Stephen had died, we turned our attention to monitoring knife crime. We learned very quickly that knife crime was a growing part of people settling their feuds or differences. Youth culture was being overtaken by a new sort of aggression that was becoming normal because of the frequency of the incidences. The severity of the injuries was also growing. The attacks were mainly carried out by young people in their early to mid-teens, and often resulted in someone using a weapon on someone else.

After setting up the charity, we decided to develop an education programme. We wanted to assist young people, through early intervention and prevention initiatives, long before they acquired the mindset that using violence was an option. We wanted to get them thinking, 'Even if I get involved in violence, I don't need a weapon. In fact, I can just walk away from that situation.' We wanted to emphasize the importance of building stronger communities, and of working in partnership with communities. In a lot of ways, what we were proposing was in response to the 70 recommendations from the Macpherson Inquiry, regarding the building of partnership with the community. You can't do effective police work on your own; you have to police with consent. Communities are essential to policing; they are our eyes and ears. Sir Robert Peel famously said, 'The police are the public and the public are the police.' The two are inextricably linked.

We had already started to work on developing a more reflective organization that could build partnerships and reassure communities, especially those that are not as trusting of the police. The more reflective of their communities the police become, the more trusting of the police those communities will be.

We saw our purpose as multi-layered: building trust and confidence in the police, building safer and stronger communities, because community is 'come-unity'. Our message was simple: let's all get together and work to reduce crime and violence, occupy public space and stand against those who are criminally minded or intimidating, manipulating or grooming people. Let's build that critical mass of people willing to stand strong in public spaces and work together – regardless of background, culture, faith or no faith.

With that in mind, we developed the Paddington Community Project (PCP), supported by the Paddington Development Trust. By this time, I had left the Positive Action Team, and was on the Paddington division of Westminster borough: one of the four sites I covered as the borough partnership inspector. I had an office in Harrow Road Police Station, and I saw that I could gain access to local communities, grassroots organizations and other statutory agencies. My role as project manager worked well, because it fitted in with my partnership responsibilities in Westminster. I couldn't have mapped things out better if I'd tried. All the barriers that could have been placed in my way had been moved before I arrived.

The project had three strands to it. The first was to get qualitative and quantitative data on what people's perceptions of safety and security were. We brought in researchers from the British Marketing Research Bureau, and they did excellent research on various strands of where communities' concerns were, relationships with police, stop and search, and how people believed they could contribute to their communities. Based on the evidence from that research, we had some evening meetings with members of the public, at which we examined what we'd learned and looked for some practical solutions from it. We emphasized the need for fellowship and the breaking of bread, by supplying a hearty meal where networking with a purpose and critical two-way learning took place. Our work was very future-focused, bringing the police and the public together. We found that when you have fellowship and break bread with people, it breaks down a lot of barriers. And so, we would serve food after these evening meetings, and the networking would continue.

Much of the learning at those meetings happened while we were eating. Everyone was relaxed, and it wasn't like being in a 'workshop' environment. It brought up some really practical solutions that I could also use to inform my partnership role.

Because we'd set up the project in response to the Macpherson Inquiry, where we had spoken up strongly, and because we felt very close to the Lawrence family, it felt natural to ask a member of the Lawrence family to be a patron. As I mentioned earlier, Stephen's father, Neville, became our patron when PCP launched in 2001. The launch was front page news on the Met's in-house newspaper, *The Job* (or *Pravda* as we used to jokingly call it).

***

At the same time as I was externally focused building bridges with the community, I was hearing internal rumours that one of the BPA's executive members was being investigated over some very serious allegations. I knew I was involved somehow, but I didn't sense that I was the main person being investigated. Nevertheless, it was occupying a lot of my headspace. And it was coming at the most inopportune time: just as I was in the process of applying for promotion to chief inspector.

As the whispers grew louder, I was busy formulating my evidence to prove that I had the skillsets needed for the new role and was ready for promotion to chief inspector. With all the work I'd been doing (running projects locally and regionally, working with the commissioner's management board and my position on the Lawrence Steering Group) over and above my role as a uniform inspector, I wasn't short of evidence to put on my application. In fact that application form was easy to complete; it just flowed. But all the time I was working on it, I had this sense, at the back of my mind, of a career-threatening problem.

I went to the assessment centre and was very proud when it was eventually confirmed that I had been placed in the top five of almost one hundred candidates for promotion to chief inspector. Being in the top five gave me such an overwhelming sense of achievement – which was replicated both at home and at our church when my promotion was officially announced. We'd started attending Emmanuel Community Church, and it's not often you have a police chief inspector on your church pews (let alone a black one). Best of all, I was told that I could stay in Westminster heading up the Partnership Unit, which meant that I could continue working on the PCP.

We rolled the project out almost immediately in early 2001. A couple of months prior to this, a young lad by the name of Damilola Taylor had been murdered in Peckham. Because the case was close to me, both personally and professionally, it had an influence on the development of the leadership programme, a key component of the PCP. A course was established for year 10 students in the four local schools to educate them on their rights and responsibilities as they developed into positive peer-to-peer mentors. Its unique components involved police interfacing with the young people around contentious issues like stop and search and other aspects of heavy-handed insensitive policing, in an attempt to offset their perceptions of feeling over-policed and under-protected.

The first leadership residential took place at Hendon that summer. We had 100 youngsters, hand-picked from four local schools: Quintin Kynaston, St Augustine's, St George's and Paddington Academy. The Year 9 heads in each school decided which of their children were best suited to take part. I led the residential in uniform, with my new rank of chief inspector. I did that so that the young people there could see me as a role model. I looked like them, and if I could do it, they could too. My background, my history, and hopefully the story of my journey (and those of my colleagues) could assist them to do the right thing. There weren't many black chief inspectors at that time; even some of the parents commented during the awards ceremony that they had never seen so many high-ranking or senior-ranking officers of colour before. I was glad to represent the Met; I've always maintained that there's nothing bad about the Met that cannot be resolved by what's good in it.

We asked the attendees to meet us at Harrow Road Police Station, and they were driven from there to Hendon. Most of the local young people would normally never set foot in Harrow Road Police Station, so this was a big ask. Even for their parents, it was quite a formidable proposition; people only went into Harrow Road Police Station if they were victims of a crime – or if they had been arrested on suspicion of committing one.

There were some very apprehensive looks on the youngsters' faces as they walked into the station on a lovely summer's day. We met them in the front office and took them into the canteen. 'You are change agents,' I said to them. 'You are young leaders. You are the first people to take part in this project, and we have faith in you.'

We started by telling them about their rights and their responsibilities and how to stand up for their rights, especially with regard to policing. We used the acronym GOWISELY to teach them what their rights were if they got stopped by the police. All officers are trained in GOWISELY; the letters stand for Grounds, Object, Warrant Card, Identification, Station, Entitlement, Legislation, Year. Therefore when an officer stops someone, they should tell them the grounds for stopping them. These could be anything from information they'd received from the CCTV footage, for example (G). Next, there's the object the officer is looking for, which could be a stolen item or something else the person shouldn't have, that's prohibited in some way (O). Even if the officers are in uniform, they should have their warrant card, which is a picture with the crest of the Met and the officer's photo, name and rank (W). Even if the officer does not show their warrant card, they must identify themselves: 'I'm Superintendent Logan (I) from Harrow Road Police Station' (S). Entitlement is next; someone being searched by a police officer is entitled to copies of the stop record (E). They're also entitled to know the legal power that gives the officer the right to stop and search (L) and the fact they have a year in which to complain if they feel they haven't been treated properly (Y).

We explained to the youngsters that it was important for them to understand police powers – but not so as to be braggadocious and appear arrogant to any police officers they came across. Arrogance begets arrogance; negative energy begets negative energy. Invariably, if you're more respectful, the officer should be too. This is an interaction in which a person can have more control by knowing their rights and responsibilities.

This also meant we delivered these components of the programme in the most objective way, even though the Met's disproportionate use of stop and search, especially on African-Caribbean men, is well documented. On average, they are up to five times more likely to be stopped than their white counterparts. The Met also has a historical emphasis on enforcement far in excess of the other constabulary areas across the country, accounting for over half of stop and searches nationally, even though it is only one of 43 force areas. It was not surprising therefore to hear the young leaders emphasize their overwhelming perception of being over-policed and under-protected.

As a result of staging the residential at Hendon, we had access to recruits who were being trained in stop and search. Getting those recruits to interact with the young people was helpful to both groups. The youngsters saw the right way for an officer to do a stop and search, and the recruits benefitted from receiving cultural feedback from the young people they would be interacting with out on the streets, once they had finished their training. Hopefully, this would enable them to see those young people a bit differently, especially if they were going to a diverse community such as north Paddington or Hackney.

Another exciting thing we did during the residential was host a video conference with groups of young people in South Africa, Jamaica, and the USA. Nowadays, people take that sort of thing for granted because you can do it very easily with Face-Time or Skype on your mobile phone. But in those days, video conferencing took a bit more effort to implement. It took us a lot of time to set up the IT logistics with the people in Washington, Kingston and Johannesburg – so much so, I began to wonder whether we were being over-ambitious. Bevan Powell did a fantastic job as our curriculum lead, which I observed regularly as project manager. I also had to ensure the technology, set up primarily by Keith Smith, was reliable and sustainable. All of this was made significantly easier by having in-house expertise within the Met BPA delivery team.

One of our aims with all this work was prevention. As a police officer, I can arrest people. But I want to prevent them from being arrested in the first place. To do that, we as police officers need to go further upstream with the people we're called to serve. We need to be involved in their education and learn their mindsets, their thinking, their reality and their identity. We realized that identity is a key thing in a young person's life, and they can easily identify with the negative things in youth culture: thug life, glamorizing gangsters, feeling that it's cool to carry a knife or run with certain people who are involved in crime, or antisocial behaviour. 'You can stand for yourselves,' we told the youngsters on the project. 'You can make the right choices and not fall into that trap of being brainwashed, manipulated and drawn into the negative spiral of crime and antisocial behaviour.'

The young people loved the video conference. Speaking to peers of similar age, they were really absorbed. We were developing positive peer-to-peer mentoring, understanding their different cultures, and recognizing that some of the young people in South Africa and Jamaica were doing some amazing things to empower themselves, with a fraction of the opportunities that their UK and US counterparts had. It was also a wake-up call for the more fortunate young people in the UK and US to make the best of the opportunities they often allowed to be squandered, or to pass them by. That really was a light bulb moment for a lot of them. Those video conferences gave them such a new look at their lives and helped them see how they had to set themselves up for their GCSEs. In those early days, we worked with Year 10 students. But after a while, we realized that it would better if we worked with Year 9s, as it wouldn't disrupt their GCSE work in Years 10 and 11. Also Bevan's lead in curriculum development was showing dividends, with the eventual formation of the unique Young Leaders for Safer Cities (YLfSC) programme that is equivalent to a BTECH level ll, where the graduates earn UCAS (University and Colleges Administrations Service) points before they start their GCSEs.

We were so proud of that first cohort. Their graduation was held in Hendon Cadet School hall and all their parents came. There was such an amazing energy and a positive atmosphere, with lively conversation and testimonies of how well the young people had done. Some of them had come to the UK as refugees from war-torn areas, and they were breaking down a lot of barriers they were facing in their education, home development, poverty, traumatized communities etc. When they received their awards, they had such a profound sense of achievement etched across their faces. At the same time, the BPA team and I enjoyed a commensurate sense of vindication: that we were on the right track, investing our time and expertise into our community with an early intervention and prevention initiative against anti-social behaviour and crime, while at the same time promoting good citizenship.

***

Our work with the PCP continued alongside the backdrop of growing 'postcode wars' that were becoming commonplace in London. We did some internal Met research around this issue, while I contacted Professor Ben Bowling at King's College, London. He showed us evidence that a lot of the territories were developed through the saturation of crack cocaine into London in the late 1990s to early 2000s. Crack was an easily concealable, easily transferable, high mark-up commodity, and it lent itself to negative peer groups on our streets, and pressure on young people in our neighbourhoods to become sellers under the control of larger scale distributors and/or producers.

Some of my officers in Paddington were stopping youngsters aged 14 and 15, who had hundreds of pounds in cash on them. The money was obviously ill-gotten gains – and at that age, they shouldn't be working anyway; they should be in school. Whenever the officers asked them where they'd got that much money from, the answer would always be the same: 'From my parents.' When we went to see the parents, they would have no idea where their children had got the cash from.

One positive in all this was that none of the youngsters who had been on our leadership programme were among the ones we were stopping and finding with this money. So at least our message was getting across. We drilled it into the youngsters on the leadership programme that there was no such thing as a free lunch. If someone's offering you a lot of money or food or clothing, or taking you out to places, they want to control you – and if you fall for it, you'll end up in that vicious cycle of decline, fear and being criminalized.

We saw our young people go from strength to strength. Even some of the feuds that were going on between some of the local schools stopped. Encouraged by the results we were achieving at a local level, we were convinced that this could work across London. We had broken down so many local barriers within the Paddington area, we were confident that if we rolled it out across London, we could break down a lot of these postcode conflicts. We had excellent results with the leadership programme for three years. The Paddington Development Trust could vouch that we were good at developing community relations, engaging young people and coming up with solutions. In fact, the Trust joined us for the award ceremony. We brought in very senior officers from Scotland Yard and the local borough

1

2

3

4

5

OCTOBER 1982

METROPOLITAN POLICE TRAINING SCHOOL
HENDON

EVERITT PHOTOGRAPHY

6

7

8

9

10

11

12

13

14

15

16

17

SUPERINTENDENT LOGAN

commander. All the things we'd done with those young people had reduced the possibility of them being dragged into a negative lifestyle. Our commitment to the community was paying off dividends, and our project team was developing. Everything was going well. And yet in the midst of all this, I had the nagging feeling that something would go wrong, which was more than a normal case of healthy scepticism or hyper-vigilance.

10

'Dad, are you going to jail?'

In December 2000, a few of us on the BPA executive were invited to a commissioner's Christmas party in his office. It's quite an honour to be invited to his party, because only senior officers and senior police staff members go to it. Being invited is a real feather in your cap. Sir John Stevens was commissioner at the time and we had a good working relationship, including his personal support for me as the newly elected Met BPA chair. I thought it was very nice of him to invite us to his party. But all through the evening, I could sense there was something not being said, because of the way some of those present appeared to be uncharacteristically ill at ease.

I was very prayerful that Christmas. It was so intense that I felt the need to fast privately to prepare myself, because I sensed the full weight of leadership weighing heavily on me. And then it happened in January 2001: I found out that Ali Dizaei – my former deputy chair at the National BPA – was being investigated on numerous issues, primarily around his lifestyle. Allegations were being made that his behaviour was not befitting of an officer. We heard of his arrest and suspension via the news media contacts, before getting a call from Sir Ian Blair, the deputy commissioner, telling us the same news.

Ali had been the life of the party when we attended the commissioner's Christmas do. He was a very flamboyant guy, very charismatic, larger than life both physically and intellectually. It was rather ironic that he was now being suspended in such a short space of time. It was catastrophic too. Some of those other party guests would have known what was about to happen, and they hadn't said a word to us. I felt betrayed, humiliated, frustrated and angry. We thought the organization had moved on, but people in it still saw minority ethnic officers as potential suspects. Once again, the Met had closed ranks on us.

Shortly after Ali's suspension, Ian Blair summoned me to Scotland Yard for a personal briefing on the scale of the allegations and the scope of investigations, known as Operation Helios. I ensured I was accompanied by a few of my executive. The summons from Ian Blair showed us this investigation had been orchestrated from the very top. Only a few weeks earlier we had shared Christmas pleasantries with him, the commissioner and other members of the management board without a word being said. Obviously, we couldn't be trusted then, but they wanted us on board now.

We were disturbed to learn from Ian Blair how the Independent Advisors Group (IAG) had validated Operation Helios. Knowing how the group was formed by the Met during the Macpherson Inquiry, I knew the members were insufficiently qualified to give accurate and objective oversight of the investigation, other than Professor Ben Bowling. He was so appalled at how the IAG was used in Operation Helios, that he immediately left the IAG.

On the instructions of Ian Blair, the senior investigating officer, Barry Norman, from the Department for Professional Standards. came to meet us at the BPA office in Pimlico and handed out copies of the allegations. It would have been easier to list what Ali Dizaei wasn't being accused of committing. Everything, bar terrorism and murder, was mentioned. I thought, 'If he was that bad and you're actually able to substantiate these allegations, why did you let it go on for so long?' They should have done something to nip it in the bud.

When Ali was released on bail, he called and during that brief discussion, I stressed to him immediately that he was a valued BPA member, and I emphasized that he would be supported, because we were standing on the cornerstone of the justice system: innocent until proven guilty. I think that reassured him.

A couple of weeks later, I then received another call from Superintendent Barry Norman. He said he would come and brief us in depth. I said, 'If you're going to brief me, you have to brief everyone on the executive.' Barry went through a whole series of allegations against Ali to kick off the meeting, followed by some clarification of the scale of Operation Helios to investigate him, which showed no expense was spared. He went on about how Ali had gone to the Libyan embassy countless times when he was not authorized to do so. He repeatedly referred to the way in which Ali conducted himself. Once again, I thought, 'If you're a supportive organization and you see someone falling out of line, then there is a duty of care to advise them, especially by his first line supervisor. Don't just let them keep running, or give them enough rope to hang themselves.' For me, it didn't add up. 'This is crazy,' I thought.

Barry Norman had come in thinking that we would just go along with his wishes and suspend Ali from the BPA. There Ali was, on the end of a branch, hanging on to his career, and we were just supposed to sever that branch and let him freefall. There was no way we were going to do that, based on the information we had heard from him and Ian Blair.

'As far as I'm concerned, Ali Dizaei is one of our members,' I said. 'We will support him because he's innocent until proven guilty. You've got to go and do your own investigation. We're not going to get in the way of that. If we're required to make statements, we'll do so. We will act totally objectively.'

The trial by media was what bothered me the most. Why had the media known about this before we had? We all knew that the Met had a reputation for leaking information like a sieve, so it wasn't surprising that this had leaked. Disappointing? Yes. Inappropriate? That too. Surprising? Not at all.

It was very tricky for us in the Met BPA executive to navigate between the investigating team on one side and Ali's defence team on the other. We had to give evidence to the investigating team, and we had to support this member of ours – all without compromising ourselves or the case itself. I felt as if I were playing three-dimensional chess with Spock from a *Star Trek* episode. I would have laughed out loud if it weren't so serious!

We called an extraordinary Met BPA membership meeting and explained to them as best as we could what was going on. Fortunately, they agreed with my rationale, even though standing up against the Met in such a high-profile case posed a massive risk to our existence as an Association.

Yet again, I had uncharted territory to traverse. That was the story of my life, getting used to exploring new frontiers. The *Star Trek* analogy is appropriate in many ways when I think of my career as a cop; for a lot of it, I was boldly going where very few had gone before.

I knew we were writing our own rulebook and changing the dynamics of the Met. And we had strong links with the media, so we were trying to put our narrative forward. Some of it was countering the Met's narrative, just to say, 'We're supporting one of our members.' That gave us a lot of credibility with the black community. People would say to us, 'You guys aren't simply falling in line with the Met; you're sticking to your principles.'

By March it was clear that the allegations against Ali were being reduced significantly, with Mike Mansfield heading up his legal team. At about the same time, we heard informally that the investigating team was now looking into the National BPA accounts in the Home Office, going back to 1998 when we formed, and I was elected as chair. We weren't surprised. This tied in with Barry Norman being very adversarial, by suggesting we would be treated as hostile witnesses if we didn't comply, when there was no suggestion we wouldn't fully cooperate. Again, it was like the *Star Trek* 3D chess: an attack could come from so many different angles. It wasn't just linear or binary; it was multi-faceted. I then realized we needed to formally instruct solicitors to represent us as an organization, so I asked Sadiq Khan of Christian Fisher Solicitors to take on this role. He had earlier approached me to carry out pro bono work, and we wanted him for Operation Helios; he had a good reputation.

Ravi Chand was now the National BPA chair. He and I worked hard; we'd known each other for a number of years before we were thrown into this investigatory maze together, and we had to figure a way out. As mentioned earlier, I first met him in 1995 when he was setting up Bedford's BPA. I found him to be a quiet, unassuming guy, very clear on what the issues were and how he wanted to play an active role. We supported each other, in a proactive and dynamic way, not only internally with our colleagues but also in terms of the public and the media. He made me feel that we were on the same page. He was a Christian as well. Having him in my corner was a godsend, and I felt even more confident in speaking truth to power on behalf of my membership, against those in seniority in the Met who wanted to wipe us off the policing map. I made it known, repeatedly to whoever enquired, that news of the BPA's demise was grossly exaggerated.

As the investigation rolled on into June 2001, it was quite apparent that the mountain range of allegations didn't stack up to a hill of beans of admissible evidence, and I was anticipating some widening of the investigation scope to justify the amount of time and money spent on Operation Helios. It presented itself loud and clear when I was on the last day of a senior leadership course, when I had a call saying that a colleague wanted to meet me in the reception. 'I wonder who that could be?' I thought. It was a Friday afternoon and we were outside London, in leafy Arundel in West Sussex. Why would someone from the Met come all this way to see me on a Friday afternoon? Couldn't they have waited until Monday morning and met me back in London? I went to the reception area and saw Barry Norman.

'Barry, what are you doing here?' I asked.

'Leroy, I've got some bad news.'

'What?'

'We've looked into the National BPA records in the Home Office.'

'Why would you want to do that?'

'We had to make sure that everything was above board. Integrity is non-negotiable.'

'Is that on your terms, or just generally?'

'Generally,' he replied.

I've never known something so extraordinary, him coming to meet me in such circumstances when he knew I was going to be at work on Monday. 'Is it that serious that you had to come and meet me?' I asked.

'Yes.'

He said he had to serve me with a Form 163: a notice of allegation against me, on a Police Regulations 9 notice – which meant something that needed to be investigated.

'Regarding what?' I asked.

He explained that it was because I had put in an application for £80 for a hotel bill, and I shouldn't have because it had already been paid for, and so I'd defrauded the Home Office – of £80.

'Are you serious?'

'Yes.'

143

I laughed (nervously, I must admit). 'Really?' I said. 'You've come all the way from London to serve that on me?'

'Integrity is non-negotiable,' he said again. He kept repeating that phrase.

'I wish it was consistent,' I replied as I took the form. 'You've got to do what you've got to do – and so do I.'

I drove back to London in a daze. I kept the car well within the legal speed limit, but my mind was doing 150 miles per hour. 'You knew this was going to happen,' I said repeatedly to myself, praying as I drove. I recalled the time I'd insisted that Gretl come with me to the Manchester BPA launch – the event for which I'd incurred the hotel bill for which I was now under investigation. I retraced all my steps. I'd put in the application for that reimbursement via the Home Office; the Home Office should have picked it up. Where could they have got it wrong? Where could I have got it wrong?

Phone calls started coming in from the community and the BPA executive, saying that some media outlets were now reporting that I was the subject of an allegation, that it was a very serious matter and it was all part of Operation Helios, the case against Ali Dizaei. Part of me was thinking, 'Wow! I'm now part of an operation!'

'They're getting desperate if they're now going to that level of spin,' I thought. It wasn't even my error; it was an admin error. But I still needed to clarify everything on my side, so I decided to get out all my files and make a thorough check as soon as I got home. There was something else I needed to do first, though...

I would have preferred to break news like this to Gretl in person, but I knew that if I waited to tell her when I got home, the media would beat me to it. So, I phoned her. 'There's a story in the news that I'm being investigated, and it's all part of Operation Helios,' I said. 'I've got to sit down with you and the children and talk you all through it, just to reassure you all that it's nothing serious.'

When I arrived home, I immediately sat everyone down and told them what had been going on at work over the past year. Myles, who was about ten years old, said, 'Dad, does this mean that you'll go to jail?'

'No, Myles, it doesn't,' I said. But the fact that my ten-year-old was that concerned that he thought I might go to jail broke my heart. The two older ones said they knew I'd be okay, and that reassured me a bit. If my teenage children could get it right, then I knew I was ok. Gretl, of course, was totally behind me – which again reassured me no end.

I then had to tell the BPA executive individually by phone – and again, they pledged their support and reassured me that I'd be fine. 'We know this is a witch hunt,' they said. 'First Ali, now you.'

The following call was to Sadiq Khan. 'I've been served a Form 163,' I said. 'Game on.' He acted promptly by informing me within a few days that if my case went to Crown Court, Matthew Ryder of Matrix Chambers had agreed to act as my barrister. This was amazing news, since I knew of Matthew's work during the Macpherson Inquiry, coupled with his very well-respected reputation. That reassured me I was on track to full exoneration.

***

After speaking to the family, I went into my study and tore the place apart looking for evidence. I searched through all my files to find my copies of expenses claims. As far as I was concerned, it had to be an oversight at most or an admin error at least. There was nothing in my actions that could be considered criminal. There was definitely an error – either on my part or the investigating officer's.

When I found my expense claim forms, I couldn't see any error on my part. I had submitted them all in keeping with the system we'd developed with the Home Office, and the invoice had been sent via the National BPA office after I attended the Manchester BPA launch. If there were indeed an error, it was with the system – not me. When I went through my records, I discovered that with all the expenses I was entitled to claim – but hadn't – the Home Office owed me about £600! I was the one who was out of pocket, not the Home Office.

That put my mind at rest. Prior to that, I'd had this lingering sense of dread. I knew the media would whip this up as much as possible, and I didn't want to be seen breaking down – especially in front of the family. It was quite stressful, anticipating the trial by media that would ensue if I were found to be at fault.

The calls from media outlets started almost immediately. I quickly lost count of the number of times I said the words, 'I have no comment at this time. This is an ongoing investigation; in future, contact my lawyer.'

Without my faith, I would have buckled. It gave me a strength, a resolve and a calmness. A lot of people commented on how I didn't appear stressed. My response was always, 'I'm too blessed to be stressed!' My attitude was: 'It's in God's hands; he'll deal with it.'

Nevertheless, I had to do my work. That weekend was one of taking stock. That and talking with Gretl – both of us coming to agreement that we would be victorious in this. It was a time of saying that whatever they were doing outside, we were not going to be moved or feel we were under siege, by standing strong on the foundation of our faith and the evidence in my favour.

Barry Norman had wanted me to be his main witness against Ali. But I'd insisted that Ali was innocent until proven guilty. It was easy to see the sequence of events that led to him investigating me too. It was quite petty, really. But it would have had massive implications if I were found guilty. I had to be prepared.

Sadiq gave me a long list of documents he wanted to see as he worked on my case. I went to the National BPA office to get some of the evidence I needed, and I consulted a lot with Ravi. We were battle-ready; we now had to have a counter-narrative to come back with.

In among the papers, I found the letter I'd written three years earlier to the then Home Secretary, Jack Straw, saying that we believed we were under scrutiny and that a witch hunt was being carried out on us. Finding that letter now, it seemed prophetic: first Ali, now me.

It *was* a witch hunt; we knew it was. Pushing the boat out the way the BPA did was always going to incur the wrath of someone higher up; there would always be someone looking for ways to exact revenge on us for telling it as it is. We were seen as whistle-blowers, as being disloyal. But my loyalty was to justice and equality. My loyalty was to people who had been victimized in so many cases, both internally and externally. When I saw that letter, I thought it could help Ali's case as well as mine. I passed it on to Mike Mansfield's team. I felt good that I'd registered my concerns. It showed that cases like mine or Ali's weren't one-offs. And knowing that, we made sure that all our procedures and practices within the BPA were fit for purpose. It was good to have that self-inventory done; it proved that we had acted with integrity within the BPA. Once I had all my material together in response to the Met, I wanted the investigating team to get going as soon as possible. Internal investigations can sometimes take years.

We had scores of supportive telephone calls and emails from various members of the community. 'We can see this is a witch hunt,' they'd say. 'Is there anything we can do?' I received a call from one of the leaders of the Nation of Islam one day. 'If you need anything, just give me a call,' he said. 'I can get a few hundred of our members to turn up outside court.' I had flashbacks of the Lawrence Inquiry, where several Nation of Islam members were involved in a violent flashpoint. I thanked him for the kind offer but graciously declined. I saw it as a positive offer of assistance in line with numerous other offers from a variety of external sources, which humbled me greatly and confirmed how the community had identified with me, the BPA movement and our stance on Operation Helios.

I got a phenomenal offer of internal assistance on the lead-up to my interview under caution the following month of July, which was much quicker than I thought it would be. Totally out of the blue, Deputy Assistant Commissioner John Grieve volunteered to attend the interview, after pulling me to one side after one of our regular Stephen Lawrence Recommendation meetings. John said, 'Leroy, you're entitled to have a friend at the interview. Do you want me to be your friend?'

I hadn't thought about it before, but when he asked, I initially thought it would be rude to refuse. Normally, your 'friend' at such a hearing would be someone of a similar rank to you, but he was four ranks above me. Also he was a nationally recognized officer for his vast experience and expertise in major investigations over decades. And additionally, he was now the public face of the police service on the implementation of the Stephen Lawrence recommendations, working towards the modernization of policing. He was making such a remarkable gesture. Taking all of this in mind, combined with knowing him for over 15 years and the fact I was currently working with him on the recommendations, I had no hesitation in agreeing to have him as my friend at the interview.

'What are your intentions?' John asked.

'Intentions? What do you mean?'

'If you've got anything to hide, shut your mouth,' he said. 'If you haven't, tell them exactly.'

In his own way, John was sounding me out to see if I was truthful and worthy of the noble offer he was making, at a risk of his personal and professional reputation. It built my faith-driven confidence to a level that failure was not an option, because everything I needed to succeed was being provided: and it didn't stop there.

I received a file from Ali's team, showing that they'd done all sorts of enquiries about him and compared them with his white counterparts, to show differential treatment. There was a file of white officers from Special Operations who had put in multiple questionable expenses claims, but they were not subject to any investigations or trial by media, not even a verbal warning. This showed a total disproportionality in the way we – as black officers – were treated, compared to how our white counterparts were. This again echoed what we'd learned from our research into the experiences of minority ethnic officers in the Met generally: black officers were six or seven times more likely to be investigated than their white counterparts.

Sadiq was elated as he read through the file, and he agreed with me the direct comparison between my case and those of the white officers was irrefutable evidence to be considered by the Crown Prosecution Service lawyers assigned to Operation Helios. I felt he was relying on me to feed him information to keep him on his toes and remain focused on my case, despite the other cases he was dealing with. I was happy to do this to ensure my name was cleared.

Despite the wealth of evidence and support in my favour, I woke up extremely nervous the morning of the interview, on Tuesday 24 July at 9.30 in the morning. I put on my bravest face to ensure Gretl and the children were not unduly worried, by cracking jokes during breakfast, then through a family prayer that reassured them they would see me later. When I left to meet Sadiq in John's office in Scotland Yard, for a pre-meet to make last minute changes to my defence strategy and to give me a confidence boost, I experienced an inner calm that took over any nerves.

After a short car journey to Tintagel House, we entered the waiting room, where the investigating officers informed me that I was not allowed a lawyer at my interview. They also questioned John's right to be there, because of his seniority, as one of the most respected and experienced detectives in the country. Fortunately, we had a clear counter argument based on my right to have the best forms of advice during the interview, and eventually the interview started about an hour and a half late. This first victory gave me a sense of control to complement the calm I was experiencing, a form of role reversal that seemed so surreal to me. Together with my formidable advisory team, I knew I was in the best position possible to deal with any questions the detective sergeant would be putting to me. I even took it in my stride when I was on the receiving end of my rights being read out by the officers during the cautioning procedure. My heart went out to the two interviewing officers, because they appeared hesitant and nervous despite their attempts to regain the high ground through some complex questions. I thought Barry Norman could have made an appearance to assist his officers and address the imbalance in my favour, but it never happened.

The interview rolled on, only interrupted by the officers replacing the audio tapes. I was asked over and over again about my time as national chair of the BPA. They were especially trying to trip me up on the events concerning the launch of the Manchester BPA, when I stayed overnight in a hotel. They asked who I was with, and I told them I was with my wife.

'What did you do?'

'We went to the launch, then came back to the hotel afterwards.'

Before I knew it, three hours had passed. I hadn't even had the opportunity to call Gretl and update her on what was happening (they take your mobile off you before you start). 'Do you know what?' I said to John. 'I've been interviewed longer than the Lawrence suspects were!' It made me wonder how many more people had been in this situation but were unable to fight their corner.

It was 6.30 p.m. when we finally left the interview room and, as we were leaving, Barry made an appearance to confirm his desire to expedite matters and to inform us that I should know the CPS decision sometime in September.

I immediately called Gretl; she was very relieved to hear my voice. 'I thought they'd arrested and charged you!' she said.

'Why would you think that?' I asked.

'You said you would only be a few hours!'

'That's what I thought,' I said.

After a short debrief, I thanked Sadiq and John for their sound advice. I was very grateful to both of them for their back-up through this critical phase, especially John whose mere presence was invaluable. He even made Barry Norman show reverence, without saying a word, which made me smile inside. I had experienced Barry at his most arrogant, when he had served the allegations papers on me. John helped to save my career, and I will always be grateful to him. In my eyes, he's a real legend!

When I finally arrived home, I was able to tell Myles that Daddy had made it through the interview.

'So you're not going to prison then?' he said.

'No, Myles,' I replied. 'All is well. There's nothing to worry about.'

It's not the type of conversation you want to have with your ten-year-old child. My teenagers, Leah and Gerad, were really concerned. Some of their school friends had read about the investigation in the papers, and they wanted to tell them that their dad was innocent. They asked a lot of thought-provoking questions about how I felt and whether I thought things were going to be all right, which I responded to with the same control and calmness that had lived with me earlier in the day during my grilling by Operation Helios detectives.

***

Not having been suspended from full-time duty during Operation Helios, I was able to redouble my efforts on my roles as Westminster Partnership chief inspector, chair of the Met BPA and PCP project manager at Harrow Road Station, where I normally based myself, to ensure I was easily accessible to the public in one of the most deprived areas on the borough. One Tuesday morning in September 2001, I was walking up to my office when I saw everyone gathered round one of the briefing room television screens.

What I saw on the screen looked like a disaster movie. An aeroplane had flown into one of the World Trade Center's twin towers in New York. All I could see was smoke and panic. And then all of a sudden, a second aeroplane ploughed into the other tower. My mind went back to the time I had been up the twin towers while on a visit to New York in the early 1980s before joining the Met. Little did I know, as we watched the disaster unfold, that it was going to affect my family.

The day after 9/11, Mum had a heart attack. We were in hospital for several days while she was in intensive care. She never regained consciousness. While we were keeping a vigil for Mum in hospital the following few days leading up to her passing, our American family were trying to call us on our landline. My uncle Roy, who lived in Fort Lauderdale, had gone to New York that day to see my cousin Lloyd. He was one of the fatalities on the ground, caught up in the subway system as the towers collapsed. It was devastating for us when we received a call from America – but especially for Dad, who'd lost his wife and his brother during the same week.

Understandably my father was never the same after suffering the double whammy of loss and, as a family, we had to come together in a more supportive way, watching him like a hawk as we brought our lives back to some form of normality. At the same time, I was totally devastated and angry that my mother had passed away while this allegation against me was still unresolved. I know it had concerned her greatly, after she had brought it up whenever she read or watched something in the media in her last few days.

Despite the time of mourning the family and I were going through, I still needed to find out what was going on with my case. A few more weeks passed, and now we really had to push to find out what the decision was. Finally, we received a pre-Christmas surprise statement saying there was no case against me. My reputation was intact; I had no further proceedings to face. Everyone at home and at work could sense my absolute relief; it was a massive burden removed. Telling Dad of the result was a bittersweet experience; even though he put on a brave face, he was understandably still pining over Mum and it showed heavily in his eyes. He was renowned for having a direct eye-piercing stare that spoke a thousand words, and it had been replaced by a mind-wandering vacant gaze.

At the BPA and Harrow Road office, the congratulations poured in. A lot of people saw me as one of the rare cases of someone successfully coming out of such an investigation not showing any wear and tear. I went to see John Grieve in his office at Scotland Yard. 'Everything's back to normal,' I said to him.

'Leroy,' John said, 'it will never be normal again. In fact, you've got to be presidential now.'

'What do you mean?'

'You've gone through such a profound experience that you need to show your calibre as a person. Your members are looking at you; your community is looking at you. You have a real role to play.'

I'll never forget that. Coming from John, it felt really profound. Hearing those words from him made me resolve to walk the talk – not to be arrogant, but to show composure and a sense of leadership, without any signs of bitterness or resentment. I distilled it down to being a 'tender warrior'.

I realized early on that legal action against the Met was important to ensure this form of disproportionate investigation, and the distress it caused, were made known internally and publicly to ensure the organization learned from it and to reduce the possibility of it happening to other black and minority ethnic personnel. Immediately, I instructed Sadiq to invoke the Employment Tribunal (ET) process by serving an ET1 form on the Commissioner Sir John Stevens. Furthermore, we were going to push for other disputes involving minority ethnic officers and staff members to be reviewed. It had become clear to me that there were other instances in which people might not have had the confidence to complain, and outstanding legal actions in which people had complained, but the Met had adopted the tactic of wearing them down. So I decided that if my case went to an employment tribunal and I was successful, the Met had to review all the other outstanding employment tribunals and civil actions.

I wasn't suing just for money but the principle of fully exonerating myself; my endgame was to highlight the institutional racism underpinning how we were being treated. Sadiq was very efficient when it came to compiling the papers for the employment tribunal, although sometimes I had to remind him that I set the strategy and not vice versa. I wasn't going to allow the 'tail wagging the dog' scenario, where I've seen lawyers setting the strategy for senior investigating officers in the Met and getting disciplinary cases horribly wrong.

After a while, I started getting calls from Cressida Dick, asking for a meeting (she was a commander at this point; she eventually went on to become commissioner of the Met). Neither of us wanted to meet on the other's turf, so after a lot of to-and-fro as to where we should meet, we agreed to meet on neutral ground at Holborn Police Station. I didn't have to be a mind-reader to figure out what she wanted to talk about.

'We would like to discuss this employment tribunal that you've put in, and see if we can come to some form of arrangement,' Cressida said when we finally met.

'Okay,' I said. 'What's that?'

She went around the houses a bit before eventually saying they wanted to offer me compensation, instead of continuing with the ET.

'What figure do you have in mind?' I asked.

'Five grand.'

I thought, 'Are you serious?' then said, 'I suggest you come back with a much better offer.' They were really just testing the waters to see if I was open to compensation. I told her that I would be – but not for such a derisory figure, and only if we dealt with the other cases.

We ended up meeting a few times over a period of three to four weeks, while Scotland Yard made its mind up. All throughout those negotiations, the prospect of an employment tribunal grew closer. We had a date set for it. The whole process felt like a game of chess. I just had to keep the momentum going, anticipating their next move and ensuring that we weren't caught on the hop.

As I hadn't heard from Cressida for some weeks, I thought we were definitely going to the tribunal – but on the day before the employment tribunal date, Scotland Yard agreed to properly compensate. I said again that I would accept the compensation only if all the outstanding employment tribunals and civil actions were dealt with, especially those involving BPA members. At that point we brought the Advisory, Conciliation and Arbitration Service (ACAS) and senior Met officers into the negotiation process. Bevan Powell was my Met BPA representative; he sat down with Scotland Yard to go through all the cases – including mine – and within weeks, they cleared them all. Some were dealt with to everyone's satisfaction and some weren't. But at least they weren't sitting in a stagnant state, slowly withering on the vine, causing people anguish and despondency.

At about the same time, Ali's case was now at the Old Bailey for very minor charges, based on expenses claims and where he reported his car was damaged. The trial was going well according to his legal team and this would account for me not being called as a witness. Instead, in his closing arguments for the defence, Mike Mansfield QC drew on the letter I'd written to Jack Straw and John Stevens in 1999, after I reminded him of it in my formal statement. In my humble opinion, I realized that Operation Helios was a total waste of taxpayers' money, even if Ali was found guilty. Fortunately, he was found not guilty, and I was pleased to have contributed to that.

11

So Solid

In 2002, Bevan Powell and I spent a few days in Jamaica, working with the BPA's partners there on our PCP leadership programme, with the intention of organizing an international youth conference in 2004. While we were in the departure lounge at Kingston Airport waiting for our flight back home, we struck up a conversation with a gentleman by the name of Rob Hallett.

Rob, it turned out, was a major player in the music industry. At the time, he was one of the senior managers of the Mean Fiddler Group, which owns some of Britain's most iconic concert venues, such as the Jazz Café in Camden. Mean Fiddler had a lot of connections with the grime music scene. As we struck up a conversation with him, Bevan and I told him about the leadership programme work we'd been delivering. This led to us discussing the grime scene and its links to crime. It was at this point that Rob had an idea. 'I would like to do a series of events across London with grime artists, advocating peace and unity,' he said.

Bevan and I thought this was a brilliant idea and decided to follow it up. While we were working on delivering a number of grime concerts simultaneously across London under the banner of Disarm (which eventually and successfully took place in 2003), with a focus on cutting gun crime, Rob introduced us to the So Solid Crew's management team, Mission Control. Over lunch, the Mission Control people explained to Bevan, Rob and me how certain So Solid Crew members were having difficulty extricating themselves from the streets. They needed to understand that what they did on stage had an effect on their street life, and vice versa.

Bevan and I held a series of workshops with the Crew at Mission Control's headquarters near the Rotherhithe Tunnel in south London. All the key members turned up including Lisa Maffia, Harvey, G-Man, Asher D and Megaman, the group's founder. I saw Megaman as a very astute businessman trying his hardest to keep his collective together. The bigger they became, the more the pressure they were under from the streets intensified. Some of that was due to envy; some was competitiveness, and some of it was a viciousness bred by some of the activities they had been involved with in the past. It was not beyond the realms of possibility that a few of them were still doing certain things that could land them in serious trouble.

Our main message to the So Solid Crew at those workshops was that they had to make the right choices in life. 'I know it's not that easy because of the situations some of you grew up in,' I'd say to them, 'but it is all down to choices, at the end of the day.' One of our biggest tasks was getting some of them to see beyond the hostility they had towards the police. One member of the Crew had never talked to a cop in a non-confrontational context prior to meeting me at those workshops. Bevan and I would say to them, 'Look – we're local; we're Londoners. We grew up in tough areas like you did. Our situations may not have been exactly the same as yours, but we were young once, and we had to deal with the police too.'

'How could you join the police, knowing what they're like?' they would ask.

I'd reply that I saw black police officers during my childhood years in Jamaica, and so the concept of a black cop didn't seem alien to me as it might be to them. They couldn't get their heads around me continuing to join the Met despite my Dad being a victim of an unlawful beating by police officers, or how he successfully sued the Met with my help. Soon the Crew had bestowed a nickname upon me: 'CI' (short for 'Chief Inspector').

The sad thing is that, despite all that Bevan and I shared with the So Solid Crew at those workshops, quite a few of their members were still unable to eschew the 'road man' life, and one or two ended up behind bars. G-Man and Asher D were both arrested for being in possession of firearms; most tragically, in 2005 Carl Morgan was sentenced to 30 years for the murder of a young man called Colin Scarlett, and Megaman was charged for conspiracy to murder. Megaman had gone with Carl to an estate in south London, where a dispute erupted, culminating in the fatal shooting. Megaman went on the run after the shooting but gave himself up shortly afterwards; it was alleged that he had told Carl to 'burn' Colin (or words to that effect) – which allegedly was not his intention.

When Megaman's lawyers asked me to give him a character reference, my first thought was that my work colleagues would not like this at all. But then I remembered something that Ron Hampton (the former leader of the US National BPA, who was giving us wise counsel) had suggested, that we might sometimes have to go against the culture of the organization in order to be objective. He then followed up with an example of speaking on behalf of an offender at odds with his colleagues and here I was in a similar position. It was clear that there would be an uproar if I gave Megaman a character reference, because it would be seen that I was siding with a murder suspect against the police. But I was giving evidence in terms of what Megaman presented to me – not what the Met might know of him – to at least give another view to the jury. There were two mistrials before Megaman was finally found not guilty at the Old Bailey. I gave evidence three times; each time I did, I would see other officers giving me the dirtiest looks imaginable.

I've bumped into various members of the So Solid Crew on a few occasions since then, most notably in 2018, when Megaman and I were both at the Greater London Assembly, giving evidence to the Police Crime Committee on violent crime. In late 2019 I attended an audience with Harvey, where he and Megaman were openly respectful of what I was trying to do in the Met and since retiring. It's always good to see them and be reminded of one of the more unusual events in my career in the Met, but within the main themes of my life and my willingness to work outside my comfort zone.

12

The Morris Inquiry

'We are ready to face down anyone who wants to carry on with witch hunts against us. We're not going to kowtow to any intimidation. And from now on, we're not going to help with recruitment any more.'

Reporters from far and wide had come to the press conference we had called to let people know where the Met BPA stood, following the Met's petty vendetta – Operation Helios – against Ali and me. I spoke at length about how tired we were of the Met closing ranks on us. We were at a resolve; we had a sense of purpose. We all believed in fair play, justice and equality. What we had realized was that even though the Lawrence Inquiry had looked into policing to some extent, there were still issues about how the organization disproportionately investigated officers of colour. It was a form of discrimination and another manifestation of institutional racism.

'So what are you going to do about it?' one of the reporters asked, during a press conference

'There's going to be a recruiting ban,' I said.

The irony was that we didn't do that much recruiting. However, the fact that we were walking and talking role models and ambassadors for the Met meant that we did have an impact. We would do some recruiting during our Revival programmes, which took place during Black History Month. We had a bus that went out to different locations across the capital with appropriate literature. So in a sense we were recruiting – including potential leaders – but we didn't do it all year round. So, when we said we were going to have a recruiting ban, we meant that we were not going to actively recruit. It sent a strong signal about what we needed, which was to get the attention of the senior officers, the Home Office and, more importantly, the wider public.

On behalf of the BPA, I approached Bill Morris, who had retired from his post as chair of the Trades Union Congress in 2003. Bill, who was now in the House of Lords, had no plans to take on any other major roles and wanted to enjoy more of his eagerly anticipated pastime of watching cricket. 'Before you disappear,' I said to him, 'could you chair an inquiry for us?' The inquiry would look at the culture of police forces in general, but primarily the Met. Bill agreed to chair it. Anesta Weekes (whom I'd met through working on the Lawrence case) was the QC, and we had the backing of the Metropolitan Police Authority (MPA), who are the Met's independent governing body.

We had a meeting with Sir John Stevens, the commissioner. Obviously, he knew about both Ali's case and mine, and that we'd called a recruitment ban, but he didn't say anything about any of those things in that first meeting. Maybe he thought it would all fade away. In fact, the ban was building momentum. People like the head of HR, Martin Tiplady, were concerned about the impact it was having on community trust and confidence, which are the cornerstones of police legitimacy. The concern wasn't about whether we went out in recruiting buses or not; it was about the optics of it and the sense of what we claimed. Also, the media had caught on to it. We had a good relationship with *The Guardian* and Channel 4 News, and they wanted to know what was going on. Before we knew it, the recruiting ban had become front page news.

A few weeks later, we had another meeting with Sir John Stevens. He'd said he wanted us to have regular meetings with him; I think that was because he bought into Don Corleone's

'Godfather' principle: 'Keep your friends close but your enemies closer.' During this meeting, someone let slip that our recruiting boycott was still on.

The commissioner was furious. He smacked the table and shouted, 'I will not tolerate this! Cut this boycott now! It's got to stop!'

There was a deathly hush until I broke the silence.

'Sir, it's not as simple as that.'

'It is! It's got to stop!'

'Well,' I said, 'we want to make sure that the lessons will be learned from all these employment tribunals. And we want to get the Morris Inquiry going too.'

'Morris Inquiry? We're not having an inquiry.'

'It's already been accepted by the Metropolitan Police Authority, sir.'

He gave me the coldest glare I've ever had thrown my way. I had to stand up to this; after all, I had my other executive members in the room. The commissioner quickly calmed down after that, but reiterated that he wanted the boycott to stop. I said, 'We just want to make sure we get this inquiry to make the root-and-branch changes the Met really needs on race and equality issues.'

We left quietly. He was okay but he was not happy. I don't know how he didn't realize the boycott was still on, because it was all over the media. Maybe he just conveniently forgot, or his advisors feared giving him bad news.

We continued with our work to get the Morris Inquiry implemented. The Met had to prepare their submission and so did other key stakeholders of the Metropolitan Police Authority, which has been in existence since 2000. It was my close relationship with the chair of the MPA, Toby Harris (soon to be Lord Harris), that made it happen, with the backing of other MPA members like Peter Herbert QC and David Muir. The commissioner and his deputy, Ian Blair, were both extremely upset about it and didn't see the need for it. But it was a necessary part of bringing about that change we wanted to see in the Met. We hadn't seen any real change in the culture of the Met since the Macpherson Inquiry. The Morris Inquiry was our way of influencing change from the bottom up.

We had to be very specific while setting up the terms of reference for the inquiry. The points that we wanted to emphasize were that it was the BPA commissioning it, that it should have an independent oversight and take into account the long-standing employment tribunals. The inquiry was going to be scheduled for early 2004. It had to take in the critical matters concerning Operation Helios in comparison to other investigations, and question whether the Independent Advisors Group (IAG) was truly independent of the Met, as it was supposed to be.

We also wanted the inquiry to look at how the Department of Professional Standards carried out its role of monitoring police conduct. What checks and balances did it have when looking at cases? How did it decide whether it was in the police interest – or the public interest – for a case to be heard? Was it really objective or even fit for purpose? Then there was the question of how the Director for Public Affairs (the Met's media wing) often reinforced certain false narratives. For instance, when I was being subjected to trial by media, there was a lot of concern about the DPA leaking information to the press. What were they doing to counter false narratives?

Ultimately, we wanted to ensure that there was a root and branch review of the policies and practices of the Met, a confirmation that proper community impact assessments were being done for these cases (and if not, why not?) and a reassurance that whatever strategy the Met employed, it should have the least amount of disruption to community trust and confidence.

Having set up our stall, we realized we had the Met in agreement. Toby Harris's personal commitment was a very strong factor in convincing the Met's senior management to work with us. It was unprecedented that police personnel had called for and got an inquiry of this nature. A lot of people might wonder why it was such a big deal for us. For me, it was about understanding that we were willing to speak up; to make sure that people knew that we weren't self-serving but were speaking about all the issues of inequality and injustice that needed to be addressed, for the Met to progress as a modern police service – one that the community trusted and had confidence in. For us, these were critical matters that needed to be dealt with.

The inquiry officially launched on 21 January 2004, and I lifted the recruiting boycott. Over a six-month period, the inquiry panel gathered evidence, received over 1,400 documents and heard evidence from 109 people over 31 days. On 14 December 2004, *The Case for Change*, the 288-page report on the Morris Inquiry, was published. Surprisingly, it shifted from its original race focus to a broader look at diversity across the board, taking in issues of gender, disability, faith and sexuality.

Never in our wildest dreams did we think we would have an inquiry of this nature. Even though it had Bill Morris's name on it, we were the main drivers pushing the agenda. And through Ravi Chand's leadership, the National BPA pushed it as well. We had made history. We felt vindicated that despite all the challenges, we were able to achieve something. We were speaking truth to power; we were getting more clarity on areas of the organization that most people would never know about. Sometimes you'd think, 'Is there any more that we don't know about how the organization operates?' (Even after I left the Met, the Special Demonstrations Squad was still investigating the Lawrences).

Sadly, none of the successors to Lord Toby Harris as MPA chair have held the Met to account in the way he did with the Morris Inquiry. This has not changed with the introduction of the Mayor's Office for Policing and Crime (MOPAC), which in my view is a huge dereliction of their duty, and it is no surprise that the Met is still institutionally racist.

13

Hackney (Round 2)

In the spring of 2004, while the Morris Inquiry was progressing, I had a conversation with my line manager, Paul Toland (the brother of Mark Toland, my former boss at Hendon). Paul was chief superintendent of Partnership for Westminster, in charge of community policing. He set the strategy, and I ensured I implemented my part of it, with a clear citizens' focused agenda, which tied in with the PCP initiative I was rolling out as project manager in Paddington at the north of the borough. We were also at the cutting edge with the introduction of Police Community Support Officers (PCSOs), deployed as extra security assets at iconic sites in Westminster, primarily in response to 9/11 and a form of reassurance to the public through high visibility patrols. When Ian Blair was deputy commissioner, he was instrumental in the introduction of the PCSOs and through Paul Toland, I was involved in their seamless integration with community officers. Eventually they were a key component of the Safer Neighbourhood Teams (SNTs) on each ward of a borough based on the 1-2-3 model of one sergeant, two constables and three PCSOs.

He was very keen for me to put in an application for promotion to superintendent; he and I both agreed that with all the experience I'd acquired, I was at the top of my game. Paul's opposite number was a chief superintendent by the name of Chris Allison. While Paul's brief was partnership, Chris was Operations chief superintendent, in charge of Westminster's enforcement teams. I knew of Chris from the early 1980s when he was a sergeant and I was a constable. He was on a TSG (Territorial Support Group), the fast response officers who respond to public order issues and critical incidents. They're specialized officers and segregated from normal general patrol officers. They responded from their own base, wherever it may be, around the Met. And they were reserved to be called upon if there were an incident on your patch. In those days, on King's Cross division, he would be the sergeant who responded. Chris had a reputation in those days for being very gung-ho, well into the macho culture. We all had our moments, but he took it to another level.

I realized that Chris must have heard I was going for promotion when he started bombarding me with emails and voicemail messages asking me to contact him. I wondered what he wanted; I had a sneaky feeling that it was to do with the promotion I was applying for. Whatever it was, I decided I wasn't going to respond in a hurry. Then one day, Chris caught me in the corridor in Westminster HQ, which is now New Scotland Yard. 'Leroy, come into my office,' he said.

'What is it?' I asked.

'I want to speak to you.'

'I can't speak right now,' I said. 'Let's make an appointment.'

A few days later, I turned up for our appointment. We went through the pleasantries and then he said, 'I've heard you're going for promotion.'

'Yes,' I said. 'Paul Toland's given me a lot of encouragement to complete my application. I believe I've got the evidence covering all the competences they're looking for.'

'I think you need more experience,' Chris said.

'Experience in what?'

'You've got the strategic competences covered but you need operational experience.'

On the contrary, I had acquired a lot of operational experience. I'd volunteered to do extra night duties as a night duty chief inspector. I was also involved in day-to-day work at Charing Cross, which was one of my offices. I made sure I kept myself up to speed on what was required as a superintendent by speaking to the officers who carried out that role. Chris listened as I ran through all this, then he said, 'I still think you need to delay it for a year or two.'

'To do what?'

'An operational role.'

'What sort of operational role?'

'I've got a role open. It's chief inspector in charge of the Criminal Justice Unit.'

The job title may have sounded grand, but the job itself was an office-bound one, making sure the Criminal Justice Unit ran smoothly from the point when officers submitted case papers. It entails liaising with the Crown Prosecution Service, making sure that all court requirements are met, and that case papers are compiled properly to be submitted to the relevant legal advocate representing the Met.

'I can't see how my operational experience will be enhanced in a role like that,' I said, to which Chris replied, 'You could do some public order work.'

'I'm doing that anyway,' I said.

'Well, you could do a bit more.'

'Thanks for the offer,' I said, 'but my line manager believes I'm good enough and I know I am, so I'll decline your offer and put in my application.'

Normally, you never decline an offer from a chief superintendent. But I knew exactly what I wanted to do. People call meetings like the one I had with Chris 'corridor conversations'. They're not recorded and are very informal, but they can have a massive impact on you because your supervisors – even the ones who aren't your direct managers – can influence your thinking and confidence. If you don't know how to stand up for yourself, you can easily acquiesce and become compliant. And then there was the racial element; would he have had the same conversation with a white counterpart? I asked him that, and he said, 'Oh, yes – of course I would.'

'Really?' I said. 'Well, thanks for the offer – but as I said, I'm not going to bother. I'll stick to my game plan. I've got all the evidence I need. If I'm not of the right standard, I'm sure the assessment centre will give me the necessary feedback. And then I might consider your offer, but I doubt it.'

Chris knew he had overstepped the mark. But I'm a great believer in not creating battles just for the sake of it; you've got to choose them and the way they are going to be fought. Besides, I already had enough battles on my hands with the fallout from Operation Helios and the Morris Inquiry. I could deal with this by myself, I decided. And the best way to do that would be to succeed with my application.

And succeed I did. I flew through the assessment process – the application, the interview, and then the assessment centre – doing even better than I expected. I knew I could do well, but you always have a little doubt in your mind, especially when someone of influence is trying to keep you down. I had a lot of support and good mentors, people like Superintendent Robin Merritt. Chief Superintendent Ron Hope, who had been the BPA's first chair when it was launched, was also now a close friend. There were several other people who assisted me, making sure not only that I put the application in, but also that it was succinct and hit all the competences – all that came across well at the interview and the assessment centre. When I got the results a few weeks later, I knew I'd done well. If you're in the top 10 across the Met, you get your postings pretty quickly as the first cohort.

I was on a day off when the results came through. It was a lovely summer's day, and I had a community meeting in

Westminster to go to – even though I should have been enjoying a break. I decided to drive down to Islington and park there. As I was going through Hackney en route to Islington, I found myself in front of Stoke Newington Police Station. This was not the route I normally would take. 'What am I doing here?' I thought, and then I felt God was saying, 'This is where I want you next.' I'd worked here before as a sergeant, and it was tough enough then. 'Lord, are you sure about this?'

I had a couple of hours to kill before the meeting. I sat prayerfully in the car. 'Lord, is this really what you want me to do?' The more I meditated on it, the clearer it felt, in a similar way over twenty years earlier that I responded to the calling of policing, taking me out of my comfort zone.

I got out of the car and went into the station. A good seven years had passed since I left, but quite a few of the people I knew from my days there as a sergeant were still around; some had left and come back with different ranks and grades. The canteen staff were the same. The station had changed a bit; the back building used to be a section house but now housed admin and support services, the Criminal Justice Unit and HR.

I was still mentally debating whether this really was what God wanted me to do. The news of how I'd aced the assessment had already reached the station. One of the chief inspectors that I knew, Pat, saw me, came up and congratulated me. 'You coming here?' he asked.

'I don't know,' I replied. 'Are there any vacancies?'

'Oh yes, there are.'

Pat mentioned that Simon Pountain was the borough commander. I'd worked with Simon before on a couple of operational matters – most notably the Hackney siege, which had happened the previous Christmas. The siege involved a 29-year-old man called Eli Hall, who had been in prison before and was known to the police for all sorts of allegations. Some officers spotted his car outside an apartment off Graham Road and went to have a look. Shots were fired and police had to cordon off the area. That was how the siege began, on Boxing Day. It went on until 9 January, when Eli ended up dead after exchanging gun shots with armed officers and setting fire to the apartment. I reacquainted myself with quite a few people in Hackney as a result of being involved in that tragic incident (in fact, my work on the siege formed part of my evidence for the superintendent's assessment process).

Pat encouraged me to go and see Simon and at least express a verbal interest. When I eventually did see Simon, we had a very productive meeting. He seemed genuinely interested in me applying for the vacancy – which, at the time, was the only superintendent role going there. I was expecting there to be more applicants for the job. Getting a superintendent's rank is tough anywhere, much less Hackney; it's a really demanding borough. Again, I thought, if it's ordained, it will happen. I put in a bid for the position in August. A week or two later, I received the fantastic news that I was going to Hackney as a superintendent.

That same month, we in the Met BPA were running and hosting an international youth leadership conference with young people from South Africa, Jamaica and America who had previously been engaged in our London programme. It was amazing to see those young people, who had previously conversed with each other via video-conferencing, coming together and exchanging ideas. Despite their differences in culture and experience, they became a cohesive group.

Things were busy on the home front as well, with preparations in full swing for Gerad's twenty-first birthday party. All my children had coming-of-age landmarks that year, with Gerad turning 21, Leah turning 18 and Myles starting secondary school.

I went to Hackney as planned in September. Just before that, we marked the BPA's tenth anniversary with an event called *A Movement in Time* at the Royal Festival Hall. We were not only celebrating the BPA's tenth anniversary but also remembering lives that had been lost through gun and knife crime, which was one of the reasons we'd developed the leadership programme. We realized that education would help our young people not to succumb to peer pressure; not to buy into thug life and gangster glamour. These memorable events were my final acts as the outgoing Met BPA chair before promotion.

I immersed myself in the work at Hackney – not only making sure I caught up with all the operational requirements and the day-to-day supervision of my chief inspectors, but also trying to get out on the streets as often as I could. Simon was very supportive. He knew I'd have a steep learning curve, and he was there to assist me. He gave me some great pointers – 'Pountain's Pointers', I used to call them. He was very physically fit; he was always into cycling and he got all the senior management to take cycling courses. Whereas in most boroughs the superintendents drove around, we cycled. It gave us an advantage; we were able to get into areas that would have been inaccessible to us if we were in cars. People who were up to no good usually weren't expecting the superintendents to be cycling about! I even gained a street nickname as a superintendent cycling round. Some curious youngsters asked me what the insignia on my uniform meant. I explained that the silver buttons on my shoulders were crowns – and from then on, my street name was 'Crowns'. I saw this as a term of endearment, in a similar way the 'So Solid Crew' had called me 'CI' when I was a chief inspector.

I found my feet and learned the operational requirements quickly. It helped that in my previous posting in Westminster as Partnership chief inspector, I would shadow superintendents in their day-to-day operations and all the different authority levels.

I needed to be up to speed on all these critical considerations in my new rank, because according to the Police and Criminal Evidence Act of 1984, the superintendent has a lot of authority regarding further detention. The way the sergeants run the custody office is heavily influenced by the critical distance with the superintendent. Out on the street, superintendents can authorize Section 60 road checks where it is anticipated that violence may occur or reoccur (depending on the quality of the intelligence), under the Criminal Justice and Public Order Act 1994 (CJPOA).

I gained a reputation for being very strict when it came to authorizing Section 60s, because I didn't want to erode public trust and confidence in police by the indiscriminate use of the legislation. In fact, one thing I'm proud of is having the lowest number of Section 60 authorizations in the Met. I didn't want to hand them out indiscriminately or give the applying officer the impression that I would just rubber-stamp their application; I wanted to make sure the officers who requested them knew what was expected of them. Any officer who wanted a Section 60 would have to be very thorough in their assessment of the incident and intelligence that would warrant having that authority in a designated area. This approach didn't make me Mr Popular, but I wasn't there to be popular. I wanted to ensure that we made that borough improve and to reduce any indiscriminate use of our powers that unnecessarily harassed any members of the public going about their law-abiding lives. I knew that whenever something went wrong with officers under my command, I would be held responsible, and it had the potential to erode trust and confidence.

I have real concerns over recent changes in the CJPOA to counter the significant rise in street violence in which the authorization officer has been devolved from superintendent, down two ranks to inspectors, because there is more likelihood of the more junior rank being less rigorous in their dealings with the applicant officer seeking the authority. This is because of the reduced critical distance between them, compared to the wider distance between the applicant and the superintendent. There have been a growing number of authorizations over the years, which have covered an entire borough instead of a designated area within it; in my view this is a gross misuse of a power that has the highest level of disproportionalities: African-Caribbean men are 25 times more likely to be searched than their white counterparts, under a Section 60. At the moment, the Met is showing no signs of dealing with this longstanding problem, and it reinforces the perception of some of the public that it's an occupying force and not a service.

Having worked in the area before, I was aware it had a bit of a bad history, with the death of Colin Roach in the 1980s and other flashpoints. I was conscious of my extra responsibilities as a black member of the senior leadership team, and as a local person who grew up in Islington and went to college in Hackney. I also knew a lot of the local people through my work with the Met BPA and the Youth Leadership Programme on the borough. I was familiar with the culture and I understood a lot of the local issues. I knew I could be a bridge between the community and the police, and with the statutory organizations there.

Members of the various bodies serving Hackney recognized this too – people such as Alan Wood, chair of the Learning Trust, which became the education department for Hackney when it went into special measures. I had only been in Hackney a couple of months when Alan asked me to replace Tony Sewell, who was standing down from his position as a non-executive member of the Trust. Alan believed that I would be a good bridge – not only with the Learning Trust and the community, but also an operational link between the Learning Trust and the police. I've always felt that we need a more holistic approach, so

Alan's suggestion resonated with my belief that education was the key to dealing with a lot of people's issues around inequality and injustice, in one form or another. Saying yes to it would mean a steep learning curve for me, even though I had been working with four Paddington schools the previous three years in rolling out the award-winning Leadership programme of the PCP, and so I accepted the challenge, even though I had a lot on my plate already.

Hackney Council then appointed me chair of the Youth Crime Reduction board. I was glad to accept this role too; it helped me in working with local strategic partnerships in a more innovative and coordinated way. Again, it showed how we could have a more joined up and less fractured approach to dealing with some deep-seated problems of deprivation and social exclusion, which manifest themselves in violence and crime.

Working with the Learning Trust was great for me, because I could speak to the heads of the schools and say, 'What can we do about exclusions?' Once pupils were excluded, they became my problem, because they were more likely to commit crime or associate with those who did so. I was eager to see what could be done to reduce that, and how my Safer Schools officers in each secondary school could assist by working closely with the staff and students. This would facilitate a joined approach with my Safer Neighbourhood Teams (SNTs), who were placed where the challenging students lived, and worked with their wider family members. Hackney was the second borough in the entire country to have SNTs after Tower Hamlets, where my old friend Dal Babu had oversight of them as the local superintendent.

My Safer Schools officers were also handpicked, each one chosen for their skills in partnership and working with communities. They were ring-fenced to each of those wards for at least two years. They were focused on the communities and had regular meetings. We acquired a lot of intelligence from those regular meetings with the community's young people and with grassroots community organizations. I'm still friends with some of those community activists to this day. Sadly, the Safer Neighbourhoods scheme was one of the casualties of austerity, over a ten-year period from 2009 to 2019. The number of officers was cut, halving the 1-2-3 model, and the remaining ones were no longer ring-fenced for community purposes or assigned to one ward but could be deployed on other operational matters off the borough. This resulted in a disconnect between the police and community, reducing the opportunities to reassure people and make them feel safe, as there was less contact time because of the erosion of foot patrols, investigations, community meetings, proactive enforcement actions... and the list goes on without signs of shortening.

I said to Simon Pountain, 'You deal with the boardroom and I'll deal with the streets.' I would work with grassroots organizations, making sure they were linked into our crime strategy. I worked closely with the Youth Offending Team (YOT) as part of my portfolio, working with 17-year-olds and below, to prevent reoffending. I also assisted the head of the YOT, Florence Kroll, in selecting managers for the team. Florence was one of my major allies on the borough, along with Dara de Burca, who worked with Youth Services. Our focus was not only being tough on crime itself, but also on its causes. How could we prevent it in the first place, with a more joined up approach at both a strategic and tactical level?

With that in mind, we developed a lot of early intervention and prevention programmes. I was able to bring the Youth Leadership Programme element of the PCP, pioneered in Paddington, into Hackney secondary schools that had a problematic exclusion rate. The young people really got into it, especially the component on how officers should carry out their functions, which I delivered. It helped them understand their rights and responsibilities better, which in turn helped them avoid getting into negative encounters with the police. The youngsters in the schools, alternative provisions and YOTs appreciated the programme, because they knew of me and what I was doing. It broke down a lot of their stereotypes around police officers of different backgrounds and cultures and colours. I guess that my African-Caribbean roots and senior leadership role removed a lot of their barriers, changing their perceptions of what they could achieve. We had some very interesting conversations and positive outcomes.

We had a lot of challenges in Hackney, but we were able to deal with most of them and that showed Hackney in a great light. One of the biggest challenges to hit us came on 7 July 2005, with the 7/7 bombings. I was due to be at a Learning Trust meeting in the city of London that morning when a call came through on my mobile about bombs going off on the Underground.

I called Gretl immediately. 'We've just heard about bombings in central London,' I said. 'Are you home?' Gretl reassured me that she was safe. Gerad had his own business and was working from home, and Myles was in school, so they were both accounted for. My thoughts turned to Leah, who at the time had an internship in central London.

'And Leah?'

'She's on the Central Line.'

Getting through to Leah was now impossible as the phone lines were all being used for more urgent matters. It was a massive relief when Gretl called about 30 minutes later to say Leah was safe. She hadn't made it into London; the Central Line had been stopped and she had to go back home.

In the meantime, I dashed back to the control room, where the scale of the problem was becoming clearer. Hackney wasn't directly impacted, but help was needed in an adjoining borough, Tower Hamlets, where Aldgate station is situated. We reassigned officers to Tower Hamlets to assist with the response at Aldgate.

The 7/7 bombings traumatized the whole community; I could see it etched on people's faces. As with any sort of bombing, shooting or stabbing, there's not only a massive impact on the families concerned, but also the wider community. In situations like that, police officers have to be a source of reassurance. We did all we could to make sure that people felt reassured by seeing the local officers on their patch. We connected with them, and they felt safe and able to work with us, especially getting the grassroots organizations to be our ambassadors.

This approach helped when Hackney was affected by another bombing two weeks later on 21 July, when a detonated bomb on the top deck of a number 26 bus on Hackney Road was reported by the driver. It actually went off when the bus was on Shoreditch High Street, but the driver didn't realize what had happened; it was only when the bus got to Hackney Road that he smelt cordite from the upper deck of the bus. By that time, we were in place to deal with it. Tension was high – understandably so, given all the deaths and injuries that happened in 7/7. Fortunately, in this instance, none of the devices exploded as they were intended to; it was just the detonators that went off. The central Counter Terrorism command was able to gather CCTV, forensic and other intelligence, which led the Met to apprehend all the suspects in different parts of the country and abroad. Even though it can be seen as a successful operation, it was severely tarnished by the fatal shooting of Jean Charles de Menezes, who was wrongly deemed to be one of the fugitives from 21/7 by officers under the command of Cressida Dick. The legacy of that tragedy is another indelible mark of mistrust of the Met by ethnic minority communities.

***

During my time as chair of the Met BPA (2000-2004), I often worked closely with the Christian Police Association (CPA).

Inspector Bob Pull was the leader of the CPA for London. He and I were on the same page on many things. We collaborated on quite a few projects, including the launch of Street Pastors – those volunteers from local churches who patrol town centres in their own time in partnership with local community cops, offering assistance to worse for wear, spilling out of pubs and clubs, and drug users. Street Pastors was introduced into the UK by Les Isaac, founder of a charity called the Ascension Trust. The concept originally came from Jamaica, where Les had observed how churches teamed up and offered practical help to people on the streets. He called on Bob and me to help in getting the infrastructure right for Street Pastors to work alongside the Met, starting with drawing up an operational business case to get the commissioner, John Stevens, and his management board fully on side. This was followed by the formulation of a project plan, and a team to develop the infrastructure to engage borough commanders, in addition to developing and delivering the training programme for hundreds of volunteers. I was fully committed from concept to delivery, and to ensuring it happened across the Met for the first five years. I knew it would show the Met the practical applications of 'faith in action' through Christians being ready to look out beyond their churches and reach out to those in need of hope and love.

Through the CPA, I also met two other outstanding officers, Tony Eastaugh and Peter Jordan. Tony was borough commander for Barking and Dagenham. Peter, like me, was keen on finding ways of encouraging churches to make a difference to their local communities. Spurred on by this, he had made contact with a project based in New York called TRUCE (To Reach

Urban Communities Everywhere), led by the Puerto Rican ex-gangster turned evangelist Nicky Cruz.

Peter brought the TRUCE team to London in November 2005, and they gave a presentation at my home church, the Emmanuel Community Church. November wasn't ideal for TRUCE's hard-hitting outreach ministry. To make matters worse, the CD that had all their material for the presentation to the church on it refused to work. Despite those hiccups, the little I did see of them impressed me enough to want to do more with them.

In the beginning of 2006, Peter and I began to work on the logistics of bringing the TRUCE team to Hackney that summer. We showed my partnership team a piece from the TRUCE CD that had refused to work last year, and they loved it. I was surprised; I thought there would be some sceptics shrugging it off, but they were all completely behind it. Maybe they didn't want to upset their superintendent. Then again, they had challenged me on other things before...

Peter was keen to coordinate the project for me, but I knew it could be a long and drawn-out process seconding officers from one borough to another. I went to Tony Eastaugh and said, 'If we can get Peter seconded, we can make TRUCE happen.' Within a couple of weeks, I had Peter seconded to work with me. That for me was a confirmation that this was going to happen. This was needed – to show the impact of 'faith in action' on reducing crime, reassuring communities, engaging with young people and, hopefully, doing some good cross-border work with Waltham Forest. It was important to me that Waltham Forest should be part of this, because of the gang rivalry across the borough border along Lea Bridge Road, and it would validate the outreach outcomes, having two sites.

Peter did a stellar job mobilizing volunteers and getting the local Assemblies of God and New Testament churches involved. The New Testament Church on Cricketfield Road in Clapton was our main base. We got our volunteers trained up, and made sure our security strategy was up to scratch and equipped to deal with any eventuality. To help with this, we brought in the Street Pastors. The local chaplain for Hackney Borough gave us the use of his vicarage as a coordination office, under the direction of Peter. It all worked together with the local authority and other public services.

We needed just over £95,000 to cover everything. We applied for funding from the Home Office, and they covered a third of our budget. That in itself was a miracle; I've never known the Home Office to support an initiative from scratch without having any previous evidence of what the project could deliver, much less a faith-based one. I would like to think my reputation as an experienced community cop in the Met was an important consideration.

Before we knew it, we were in July. The TRUCE team came over first, with Nicky due to join them three weeks later. The first estate we hit was the Jeffrey Estate on Falkirk Street in Hackney. I knew the area well; the estate was right opposite one of the sites of Hackney Community College, where I'd taken my A Levels. I wanted to launch the project in an area I was comfortable with, and no area fitted the bill like Hackney (where I worked) and Waltham Forest (where I worshipped and lived). I felt those two worlds of my personal and professional lives colliding again, but this time I felt more in control: I wasn't walking on eggshells.

We had to get permission to play recorded music in an open setting and did live shows using backing tracks. The TRUCE team wrote music especially for the programme, and so they came over from New York with a brand new CD of previously unreleased material that they'd written and recorded, including a couple of tracks made in collaboration with my elder son, Gerad, an up-and-coming record producer, song writer and performer. The CD never went on commercial release, so those who own one have a collector's item on their hands.

I felt so blessed that other family members were committed to the initiative, not only in their prayers but also in their time, starting with Leah, my daughter, working with Peter Jordan in catering for the day-to-day needs of TRUCE, and Gretl as an outreach volunteer. Beyond my relatives, it was a real family affair, brought together through a growing fellowship with a God-given common purpose.

The TRUCE team had to talk us through their method of working. We arranged a picnic for all the volunteers, the stewards and Street Pastors. Nearly three hundred people turned up to a Christian camp just outside Chigwell, where the team were staying. The team leaders, David Ham and Patrick Dow (Nicky Cruz's son-in-law), talked us through the process. TRUCE called their modus operandi 'Hit and run'. The team would go to an estate, turn their music on, then go up to people and give them flyers and say, 'We've got a live event in the next 15 to 20 minutes. Come on down!' I think that their reputation and being American attracted more people than a local outreach initiative would have done.

I researched each estate or area the team was going to. If a negative peer group or a gang had a presence in the area, I'd make sure the team had prior knowledge of that, so they wouldn't be putting themselves at any sort of risk. More importantly, they knew who to talk to in order to obtain permission, so to speak, to operate in that area. It's a 'street code' type of thing: 'We know this is your area where you live and/or operate; we want you to know that we're not here to create any sort of problems for you. We're just here to do our thing.'

The team would get the nod; they would then start the music, hand out the flyers and invite people to the street service on their estate, park or neighbourhood. Young people loved the sound and the beat of the music. It was dynamic, current and relevant. And it was brand new, produced specifically for this initiative. When they had enough of a crowd, they would do a 20-minute show. In between songs, they would give spoken testimonies of how they'd gone through the school of hard knocks and how their faith had helped them through. It created a sense of ownership among the youngsters from the estates; they called the team their TRUCE team. That created such a buzz of joy and friendship.

The week before we went to the first estate, a horribly grotesque murder had been committed there. The victim was known to be involved in criminal activity, but the way he suffered was just horrendous. It was as if the killers were using him to send out a message to other people. You could see that there was going to be some retribution. The young people were affected. They would go straight home from school, and wouldn't go to the youth clubs as they normally did. Their parents were also scared. Obviously, I had to be careful bringing the team into a volatile situation – especially for their very first event.

You could sense the atmosphere on the Jeffrey Estate change the moment the team started to play their music. The young people were pensive and tense at first, but their curiosity got the better of them and they came out to hear the DJ and see the team's body-popping display. And their parents also sensed that the TRUCE team and their people were safe for their children to be around. It felt like carnival had come to Hackney. The main difference for me was the absence of wall to wall officers being present. I only allowed the volunteers, stewards and street pastors to have a uniform presence in their T-shirts to work with my SNT officers assigned to that ward. I had back up officers secreted in surrounding streets who could be called upon if larger number of officers were required to deal with a critical incident.

After the TRUCE team had done their captivating ministry of music, song and dance, they had a laser-like accuracy in speaking to the people who I anticipated were at high risk of harm and stayed away from those who posed a direct significant threat to members of the community. This was followed by our other outreach team volunteers, who chatted with the young people in the audience, to get a sense of what their needs and aspirations were. Some wanted to get back into education or go to college. Some wanted jobs; others wanted help dealing with alcohol or drug problems. Some wanted guidance on how to start a business. The outreach volunteers listened to them and signposted where they could get the help they needed for whatever needs they had. We got them to fill cards with their contact details, so that we could follow up with them after the TRUCE team had gone, and continue helping them move on with their lives.

Having it go so well on the Jeffrey Estate was a huge encouragement. Not one negative incident or disturbance happened throughout that whole time. This was replicated in Waltham Forest within the first week, and the Beaumont Estate was no exception. There had been a lot of tit-for-tat conflict between negative peer groups in Hackney and Clapton; the E9 gangs and the Beaumont Crew in Waltham Forest. Lea Bridge Road connected the two, and that's where they would have their flashpoints. The Homerton Crew and the Beaumont Crew were also always at odds with each other; they were constantly having stabbings and even shootings.

We still had our surveillance teams monitoring gang activity, as well as our uniformed officers. They noticed that some of the young people who would normally be adversarial on sight were seen talking to each other – gangs who would normally be at each other's throats with weapons or fists. The London Fields gang were seen speaking to the Holly Street gang. It came as a surprise when we started to observe members of the Holly Street and London Fields gangs in the same area but sitting down, talking without any hint of violence. It could well be that they were collaborating to do bigger jobs, but it was unheard of for them to be in the same space without violence. Again, that showed a remarkable change in behaviour and a reduction in crime.

In the three weeks, some 1,800 people asked for help with one issue or other. We were only in the area for a short period of time before moving on, but we were able to refer them to public services who could help in the long-term. The statistics covering that period in Hackney showed a marked fall in gun and knife crime by 30 per cent. Woundings and street robberies dropped by about 15 per cent.

The TRUCE events not only helped us reach out to the local young people, it also gave us some valuable police intelligence: for instance, we were able to gather evidence of the Holly Street gang's crack-dealing. It was proof that if you make the public feel secure and respond to their needs, you can have amazing results. Again, it showed faith in action. Some estates we visited more than once because of the demand from the residents.

Those three weeks zoomed by. Before we knew it, Nicky Cruz was due to arrive, but just before that, I started to hear comments from a Hackney journalist that TRUCE was seen to be homophobic. I knew we hadn't had any such problems on the ground, but we found out that certain people from Hackney had gone to Nicky Cruz's website – which, obviously, is coordinated in America where attitudes around certain issues can be quite cut and dried. Some people in Hackney argued that if Nicky said that being in a gay relationship was a sin, then anything to do with him must be homophobic as well. This massive leap was initially made by the *Hackney Gazette* on its front page, which said TRUCE was homophobic and was on our estates, indoctrinating our children. When they found out I was involved, they turned on the police, asking how we could sponsor such an event. This trial by media had a sinister feel reminiscent of the investigation against me, a counter-narrative to our very successful faith-based initiative. It was quite clear that if we were doing the Lord's work, there would be a backlash against it – and us.

Meanwhile, there was no such reaction in Waltham Forest. They were seeing similar headlines, but Waltham Forest Council did not say one word of objection, publicly or privately.

Jules Pipe, the Mayor of Hackney, called me for a meeting. 'You should stop this initiative of yours because it's homophobic,' he said.

'Show the evidence that it is,' I replied.

He said someone had gone on to Nicky Cruz's website and asked for advice, claiming to be in a same-sex relationship. Nicky's people had responded, 'Leave that sinful relationship' or words to that effect. This was now being used as evidence, even though there was no evidence of it in any of the TRUCE team's events here – neither in Hackney nor in Waltham Forest. I was glad I'd made the decision to work across two boroughs. It gave me something to compare Hackney against, and put it in context.

It was obvious that the mayor and the chief executive of Hackney, Tim Shields, had their own agenda. The problem for them was that I was able to show that they had signed off on all my initiatives. I hadn't done all this on my own; the local strategic partnership team was involved, as were the local authority, Youth Services and the Learning Trust, of which I was a non-executive director. This was legally airtight, and that's what upset them: they couldn't get out of it unless I agreed to it. I told them point blank that I wasn't going to.

Waltham Forest was calm and were getting on with it. I said to the mayor and his CEO, 'Why isn't Waltham Forest's borough commander saying anything?' They couldn't answer.

The meeting with the mayor and his people felt like an inquisition. I sat at the end of a long table, and they fired questions at me nonstop. 'I hear what you're saying,' I said to them, 'But there's no evidence for it. I understand that certain things may have been said in America, but it's a huge leap to assume that something similar is happening over here, because there's nothing to suggest that it is. If there was, I would stop it. And in all honesty, I think you are overreacting, when I compare your actions to Waltham Forest. They're a local authority just like you, but they have not made any complaints.' They could not respond to me.

'Here's the paperwork,' I continued. 'You all signed it off. So please tell me why.' I made it abundantly clear in a composed manner that I would prefer to leave the Met Police, rather than stop my mission. They just looked at me, thinking 'This man's a religious fanatic.' I could see it in their faces; they thought I'd lost it.

As I left the meeting, I knew that I had to say it as it is, just as I had before the Macpherson Inquiry. I knew they would try to close ranks on me. I also knew that I wasn't going to get any further promotions within the Met. Whatever I was going to do from now on, Hackney's Mayor would oppose me in any way possible; Jules and Tim wouldn't take it lightly. But I was comfortable in my own skin with the rank I had and clear that if one door closes, another will open, even if I had to make my own door. They might want to stop things, but if God wanted me to do something, no one could prevent it. I could see that; I just had to make it clear. It was a sacrifice I was 100 per cent ready to make. I still had seven years to go in the Met. But if it had to be, it had to be. It wasn't just about position rank-wise. It was more about my position in terms of influence, and about being authentic – to my faith, to what my purpose was, to being seen as a person who wouldn't just run away and cower in a corner. I had to have that warrior spirit. If I hadn't had it, I would definitely have succumbed to the pressure. Fortunately, I was supported by so many people praying for me. It was the same as when I was being investigated. So many people called or sent emails and text messages saying they had me in prayer.

Gretl was totally behind me. Anyone else would have said, 'If you walk out on this job, how are we going to pay the bills?' Not Gretl. Her attitude was that God will provide and there will be no lack. 'We are the head and not the tail' is the line she always gives me, in her Nigerian fire-and-brimstone-preacher style.

The national media, both press and TV, heard about our work. It culminated with the BBC sending their presenter Brenda Emmanus to Hackney to ask us what we were doing. I told her about our 'Five Es' engagement strategy and how the project was helping reduce crime and repeat offending; how we were getting intelligence of who was doing what (and where) to inform our enforcement proactivity; how people were feeling more secure in using public spaces again, rather than being imprisoned in their own homes.

And so, we carried on. Nicky Cruz arrived in London amid a hailstorm of media coverage. Most of it was positive; the negative reports were mostly confined to Hackney, especially the *Hackney Gazette*. The criticism was manageable, especially when you had Waltham Forest to compare it against. There was no negativity at all from there. That was my biggest defence: why are you in Hackney so against what we are doing, compared to Waltham Forest? In that sense, doing cross-border work really paid off. If I'd been confined to Hackney, I probably would have been forced to bow to pressure and pull the plug on my initiative.

People kept asking when the next event was. We told them we were going to have two scheduled concerts at the Ocean theatre in Hackney, which is now an Odeon cinema. The concerts were free, but people still had to book tickets; both concerts sold out. Nicky was amazing and we had a terrific response. While people queued up around the building to enter the concerts, the media were interviewing them, and it was clear they were not usual church folk attending an outreach service, but local people responding to a desire for change through a unique form of evangelism. This reflected in the standing room only services and the altar calls, where hundreds of people came forward.

Other than working collaboratively with churches, street pastors and public services, we ensured our work also dovetailed seamlessly with other outreach programmes. The main one covering east London at the time was 'Soul in The City' picking up where we left off in late July and pushing through into August, coordinated by Patrick Regan and Tanya Bright. We had a phenomenal church service that attracted a large crowd of young people, who had responded to TRUCE and were encouraged then to support Patrick, Tanya and their team as they kept up the message of hope that people were willing to respond to if it's put across in a relevant way.

I didn't want TRUCE to disappear without a trace, and I launched a faith-based social enterprise called REALLITY – Raising Everyone's Awareness of Lives Lost in The Youth – with a focus on community engagement, especially with young people. The REALLITY social enterprise was meant to be a London version of TRUCE. We developed our own homegrown outreach team and had some great people, the team including my son Gerad (Creative Co-ordinator) and my daughter Leah (Outreach Co-ordinator). The Gospel rapper Guvna B was with us in the initial stages. TRUCE was a family affair, and REALLITY was the same. The trustees include

Bevan Powell, who worked extensively with me in the BPA, and Rob Neil, my old friend from my time at the London Church of Christ and All Souls Langham Place. We couldn't have done it without the help of Dr Richard Stone, who had been on the panel for the Macpherson Inquiry. He provided us with much-needed office space and financial support.

REALLITY might never have prominence, but we're doing the work that God put in our hearts that we need to do – not only at a grassroots level but also at a strategic level, drawing together our collective expertise of over 70 years in the justice system and how it impacts communities.

***

I was putting in very long hours – in my day job, in my work with the Learning Trust, as well as other statutory and voluntary sector organizations I was involved in, as well as developing an anti-gang mobile intervention team, together with Florence Kroll, head of the Youth Offending Team; and working on stamping out the crack distribution on Holly Street and other parts of Hackney. There had been a number of shootings at the local nightclub called the Palace Pavilion, and I was busy gathering evidence to have it shut down. We were getting a lot of helpful intelligence. That stretch of Lower Clapton Road had acquired the grisly nickname 'Murder Mile'. I had to deal with that.

The club's owner, Admiral Ken, had a security problem, but he wasn't dealing with it. It was attracting people from all over the south east and other towns and cities across the country who had feuds. It had become the place to come and assassinate someone. The weapon of choice was semi-automatic guns. I warned Admiral Ken that if it continued, I would close it down. My issue was not just that these events were happening, but that when my officers went to investigate, Admiral Ken and his staff would act as if the place was closed. On one occasion, the officers entered the place and it was packed – but the staff turned off the lights and the music, and people were hiding in there. We'd just had a shooting, and they were giving us the 'hear no evil, see no evil, speak no evil' act. What sort of nonsense was that? It had to stop. I had to respond to the outcry of the community. In the end, I was able to use the current Licensing Act of that year (2006) to close it down. That reduced the borough's gun-enabled crime figures by 40 per cent – just by closing down one venue!

***

I co-ordinated the production of a full report of the TRUCE team's outreach, including a DVD and an analysis of the outcomes. I took copies with me to New York for the TRUCE team, and we had a great time reminiscing about all that had happened that summer. The team said that none of the other people they'd done outreaches with – whether locally or internationally – had ever given them such comprehensive and evidenced feedback on their work. It was clear we had struck up meaningful relationships, not only because of our successes but also the challenges we had to face, which built our confidence and character in our faith in equal measures.

I was with TRUCE in mid-December, after which the plan was for me to meet up with Gretl and the children in Jamaica, where we would spend Christmas together. I flew from New York to Jamaica on 20 December, but on arrival I felt really ill. I had no idea what was wrong; I felt absolutely exhausted, but I thought that was just down to overwork.

On the day I was meant to pick up Gretl and the children at Montego Bay airport, I received a phone call from her, saying that the flight had been cancelled because Heathrow was engulfed in thick fog. We were flying Air Jamaica. It's not a big carrier, so if you miss your flight, it's almost impossible to get another. Gretl and the children spent three days going to and fro between the airport and the hotel they were staying in, spending hours at the airport waiting for a flight that never came. Finally, on 23 December, Gretl called and said, 'We've got to cancel this. I can't put the children through this any more.'

'That's ok with me,' I said. 'I'm coming home, and I'm not feeling very well either.'

I still had no clue what the problem was. I put it down to the volume of work, because it had been a really demanding year – not just physically but spiritually too. With all that pressure going on in my life, I felt it was only natural that something had to give.

Gretl suggested I stay in Jamaica, but there was no way I was going to stay there on my own over Christmas. The trip was insured; we would just try again next year.

I got one of the last flights back to the UK. All during the flight, I felt a heavy pressure on my chest and found it difficult to breathe. I still didn't think I was suffering from anything specific; I thought it was just cabin pressure and I would be okay once I got home. I arrived at Gatwick and caught the train. I called Gretl and said, 'Please meet me at the other end. I'm feeling really exhausted.'

By the time I got there, I couldn't even carry my suitcases. Out of nowhere, a guy came up and said, 'Can I help you, mate?' He helped me go up the stairs with my luggage and walked with me all the way to the car.

Gretl was really concerned when she saw me. 'You look terrible,' she said. 'What's the matter?'

'I don't know,' I said. 'I'm just very exhausted.'

My breathing was very shallow by this stage, but I didn't want Gretl to panic. I still thought that all I needed to do was get some rest. When we got home, Gretl had to help me get the cases out of the car, and I went straight to bed.

In other circumstances, that could have been my last night. But praise God, he maintained me. The symptoms persisted all the way from the day before Christmas Eve to Boxing Day, and by then I couldn't walk up the stairs in our house without puffing and panting. I felt twice my age. My legs were heavy, and my lung capacity was so low I couldn't hold my breath properly. I still couldn't figure out what it was. I'd been exhausted before, but never like this. I decided to call the doctor first thing the next morning.

The doctor ordered me into the GP practice, giving me a full examination, and asked if I'd ever had these symptoms before.

'No,' I said.

'Any other symptoms, other than this laboured breathing?'

'I did feel a localized pain in my left leg.'

He examined my left leg. 'Have you ever suffered from deep vein thrombosis?' he asked.

'Not that I'm aware of,' I said, 'but my dad died from it four years ago.'

'Right,' he said. 'You're going straight to hospital.'

I was admitted within hours. The hospital staff did a whole battery of tests, and found that I had suffered pulmonary embolisms. Instead of the clots caused by the thrombosis going to my heart (which would have been fatal), they went to my lungs and were now spreading.

I spent four days in hospital, and was put on blood thinners. I'd had a very close shave. Those clots eventually do end up in your heart. If I'd stayed in Jamaica, I could have collapsed alone in my hotel room and anything could have happened. If Gretl's flight hadn't been cancelled – which was just as miraculous, when you think about it; Heathrow rarely has fog like that – I could have died in my room waiting for her flight to arrive. I felt very blessed. Things could have been so different. But it showed me again that any further promotion I would have in the police wasn't going to be through the ranks.

As 2007 rolled in, I had some thinking to do. I knew I couldn't stay at Hackney after the row over TRUCE. I was getting over the pulmonary embolisms, and we had our third commissioner's commendations for best performing borough, especially after TRUCE and the subsequent crime reductions we'd experienced. I had to progress my career elsewhere. I knew I couldn't go for any more promotions. I wasn't physically ready for them, especially after the embolisms. I was the walking wounded for many years in my career, what with the back injury and the broken ankle. But you just get on with it. With the pulmonary embolisms, however, I realized I couldn't put myself in a position of even greater responsibility in a borough as a chief superintendent. Even though it wasn't directly work-related, it had happened because of my workload. Putting myself forward for a higher position wouldn't be fair on someone else who not only had the mental capacity but also the physical capacity to deal with it. Mentally, I was fine; physically, no. I had to be wise; whatever advancements I made now, they would have to be lateral in terms of ranks. If I was consistent, I would have a voice that would be heard. I would have a platform wherever it was appropriate to have one.

People would say to me, 'I hear you're leaving Hackney'. I hadn't said I was, nor had I applied for any jobs outside. But the turnover for senior leadership in a borough is two to three years and I was coming up to the end of my third year at Hackney, so it's easy to see why people thought I was going. By the summer of 2007, I'd decided it was time to move on.

One day, I had a meeting with assistant commissioner Tarique Ghaffur, my former boss at Westminster. It was a Met BPA-related meeting; I still did things for the Association and so did he. I said to him, 'Boss, I'm thinking of moving on from Hackney. Can you suggest anything?'

'Sure,' Tarique said. 'Come and work with me on the Olympics!'

14

London 2012

I did have a strong sense that the 2012 London Olympics and Paralympics would be my next step and when Tarique said he wanted me to lead on community engagement, it was too good an opportunity to pass up. Community engagement was my strength, and to do it not just in London but also at the different sporting sites across the country was another opportunity to re-establish links with contacts made during my time as chair of the National BPA. I had now spent 24 years in police service, and I felt the Olympics would give me an opportunity to maintain my development, working at executive level on a once in a lifetime event. If it went well, I would be able to leave the service on a high. It took a few weeks for me to give my notice in to Hackney and make my fond farewells to friends and colleagues alike across the borough, culminating in a tearful leaving reception at Hackney Council Voluntary Services, hosted by Jake Ferguson, their CEO and emceed by Florence Kroll. The good thing was I still had links with them as a local person, volunteering my time in the charity sector, and Hackney was also one of the Olympic boroughs.

Tarique's team had a small office on Cam Road in Stratford, not far from the Olympic site. I had a small team of three other officers, an inspector and a couple of PCs on attachment, a massive reduction in personnel under my command. My partnership unit had been made up of over 150 officers. The site was literally a hole in the ground at the time; it was the biggest excavation site in Europe.

The soil in the area was found to be toxic, and so it had to undergo a unique cleaning process before any building work could begin. They cleaned and decontaminated so much soil, they donated the surplus to local allotments and golf clubs for free. The London Organising Committee for the Olympic Games (LOCOG) used to put on tours of the site for staff and their friends and family. I took my family to see how the soil was being purified. Myles was unimpressed. 'I've never seen so many different shades of dirt!' he said when I asked him what he thought. He's always been a young man of few words! I felt the need to put it in context for him that prior to being the Olympic site, it had been a collection of industrial warehouses that invariably were used for rave parties, one of my crime hot-spots for drug supply and firearm offences. I think he eventually agreed with me the site was an area of new beginnings that had the potential to transform east London, which he would benefit from as a local person growing up in the area.

There were no major challenges that first year, other than my first day on 5 November 2007 when a small unsuspicious fire ignited on the site; I realized it was Guy Fawkes night after all and they wanted to welcome me with a bang. However, it was a totally different issue for Tarique, who sensed that he'd been overlooked for promotion and wasn't being treated the same as his white counterparts. Relationships broke down between him and the Commissioner Sir Ian Blair, and he was subsequently relieved of his post as head of the Olympic Coordination Team. This was followed by an out-of-court settlement and his eventual departure from the Met under full media scrutiny.

To my amazement (and horror), Tarique's replacement was Chris Allison: the former chief superintendent who had previously tried to stop me from applying to become a superintendent. With four years to go before the Games, it looked as if my days on the Olympic Coordination Team were numbered.

I was certain that Chris and I would fall out over something at some point. The mental jousting with Chris defined my time working on the Olympics. I was always aware that he or someone else might want to move me on to something else. Whenever I had to give a verbal report to Chris at programme management meetings, he never questioned any of the updates I gave. I didn't know whether he was wary of being confrontational or just didn't want to upset me; he can be quite an abrasive person when he wants to be, but he treated me with remarkable tact. I liked it that way and I knew it would be an interesting four years, if I lasted that long.

When Chris had fully settled in, he totally restructured Tarique's strategy. Every six months, the leaders of the Olympic Coordination Team would change things round and give us different responsibilities. There was a lot of chopping and changing. In a way, the London Olympics was like Brexit: the people leading the campaign for it didn't think they were going to get it – and then when they did, it was 'What do we do now?' There was a lot of starting things and then stopping them: doing something new, then going back to the original plan. Not even the government seemed to have a clear idea what they wanted. It was a massive undertaking, not just for the Met but for other forces around the country – as far as Scotland and the southern tip of Cornwall, where the yachting events took place.

I was in charge of community engagement around the Olympics site for a couple of years: keeping communities informed, letting them understand that things were not going to happen against their will, and that whatever did happen was going to be for the long term and provide a legacy to the community. There would be massive job opportunities leading up to and during the Games, and after they were over, to assist in community cohesion.

The senior leadership of the Olympic security team changed with monotonous regularity, and this caused a lack of grip in the early stages in crafting the security strategy and the financial package that went with it. One of the greatest threats to the Games was terrorism, and Charles Farr, the leading light of the counter-terrorism strategy Contest was appointed as the director of OSCT (Office for Security and Counter-Terrorism). I had my doubts about him. He lacked credibility and was called 'Charlie Farley' behind his back, but actually I was surprised by his performance. Even though he wasn't a charismatic figure, I found him interesting, primarily because of his eye for detail and a thorough understanding of the 'look and feel' of the security strategy.

It did come as a shock, however, when the media announced that missiles were to be sited on the rooftops of tower blocks surrounding the Olympic stadium in east London. That was so bizarre. I remember hearing they were doing that and thinking, 'Come on, guys!' I know terrorist incidents have happened before at the Olympics (most notably the 1972 Munich Games), but it seemed a bit extreme. Siting missiles in east London was definitely beyond my pay grade. I never saw the risk assessment on that level, which I'll put down to my glass half-full mindset. If these missiles had been launched, there would have been a great chance of public casualties, as we have seen in urban conflicts around the world, and this created unnecessary fear in the public. Fortunately, the missiles were never needed.

With the Joint Intelligence Committee, the GCHQ people, the senior Home Office and security services people all together in one room, there was a strong public school old boy network atmosphere. As a comprehensive school educated, non-Russell Group university bod, I may have been perceived as being out of my depth, but I wasn't concerned, knowing I had a good understanding and cultural awareness of the diverse communities impacted by the security plans. It was a learning experience to hear these people discuss the 'Five Eyes': the alliance between the intelligence services of Australia, Canada, New Zealand, the UK and the USA. I came to appreciate the importance of those alliances and of working closely with Interpol and the European Union. I could see that our security strategy couldn't be done in isolation. We needed to be able not just to pick up intelligence, but to prevent things happening in the first place. This is why I voted to remain in the European Union; unless you see these links at work in a real, dynamic way as we did during the Olympics, you'll never truly appreciate how important our international alliances are to keep us safe and secure.

In 2009, we moved from Cam Road to the seventeenth floor of the Barclays Building in Canary Wharf. LOCOG's office was two floors above us. All the other agencies were in the building too, so our work became a lot more joined up. Everything was 'London 2012', and it's where we were given our final name as the Olympic Policing Coordination Team. It was good to be able to say we were part of the Olympics and Paralympics, as the big event drew near.

The excitement and anticipation on Floor 17 ramped up even more after the Beijing Games took place. We learned a lot from Beijing – though in my case, the learning happened from a distance. I was meant to go to Beijing with a team of colleagues, but Charles Farr was instructed to cut the team down drastically, and I was one of the casualties. This was where I began to see the direct effects of austerity kick in, especially reducing the national security costs from approximately a billion to around £450m.

Once the torch went down in Beijing, the build-up to London 2012 began with a vengeance. Suddenly it was all happening: the complexity of the plans, the intricacy, the detail and the International Olympic Committee (IOC). The IOC were a unique group of people to work with. They had diplomatic status, and they carried themselves as if they owned the place. Once the venues were built, the IOC people really imposed themselves. It was like the circus coming to town, except that this circus took two or three years to turn up, was present for just two months and then moved on, even though they were very interested in the sustainability and legacy plans for the Olympic sites across the country.

All of a sudden, people you thought had moved on from the Met returned as 'consultants': a lot of former police officers and several ex-Home Office officials. Everyone in power wanted to leave their mark on the Olympics. Boris Johnson was elected Mayor of London in 2008; he left his mark with that monstrosity of a tower in the Olympic Village and the money-losing cable car running from North Greenwich to the ExCel Centre. Theresa May became Home Secretary in 2010, determined that the Games should go as she wished. There were just too many cooks, and I don't think they got it, especially the legacy aspect of it. In my opinion, that was why in the end it cost so much to convert the Olympic Stadium into a football stadium for West Ham.

Our brief included the Westfield shopping mall in Stratford. Westfield had been planned before the Olympics, but once London won the bid, work had to be coordinated with the Olympic site. We had to secure the site, and we had Gurkhas working the security there. The Gurkhas were amazing. They were very focused; they would stand on point and wouldn't leave. They would challenge anyone who wasn't meant to be on site – especially in the early days, when it was just 'piles of coloured dirt', as Myles put it.

The only hiccup leading up to the Games was the huge blunder G4S made regarding the security personnel. G4S seemed to be under the impression that you could train people two to three years before the Games, and those people would undergo the training, get their qualifications and then hang around on standby waiting for the Games to begin. Most of their applicants thought, 'Why wait two years for a job that will only last a few weeks? I'll get the training, get a qualification, and then go and find a job immediately.' Anyone could have seen what was going to happen. We had already decided that we would call on the military to mitigate that risk once we realized G4S were totally out of their depth. The military filled in seamlessly.

***

As my work in the run-up to the Games went on, deeply rooted inequalities became more evident. You would say to someone, 'The Olympic Games are for us', and their response would be, 'That's all well and good, but I can't pay my rent and feed my children this month – and yet there's this multi-million pound stadium being built on my doorstep.' I encountered that so many times. I still had my BPA hat on, and the BPA were doing a lot to build links with the community. I saw this in my REALLITY work too. We were based in Stratford and were doing a lot of outreach work. We would try to engage young people who lived right in the shadow of the Olympic stadium, but they might as well have been in another universe. They were living in fear of crime, with a lack of hope and aspirations.

All that disillusionment would find an outlet in the most explosive way just a year before the Games. On the evening of Saturday 6 August 2011, I was at home, relaxing at home with my two sons, when one of them picked up his Blackberry and said, 'Dad, Tottenham's burning!'

Two days earlier, police officers had shot and fatally wounded Mark Duggan, a 29-year-old man, on Ferry Lane in Tottenham. That Saturday afternoon, about three hundred people marched to Tottenham Police Station, saying they wanted justice for the Duggan family. What started off as a peaceful protest soon escalated into a riot – which, over the following days, sparked off copycat riots across London.

The 2011 riots didn't happen overnight. The killing of Mark Duggan became a catalyst for underlying community unrest, focusing on some issues that hadn't been addressed – maybe even going as far back as the 1985 Tottenham riots and the deaths of Cynthia Jarrett and PC Keith Blakelock (Duggan was a recognized figure in the Broadwater Farm community, where that riot had started 26 years earlier). It was an open wound that hadn't healed, and the killing reignited everything. If you don't deal with things like these, they will come back to haunt you.

Things could have been so different in Tottenham that weekend if the police had attended to the Duggan family in a more culturally competent manner, immediately after their son's death. Instead, we heard many stories of the Duggan family leaving Tottenham Police Station, upset because they didn't get the information they wanted about Mark's death. If I had been the borough commander, I would have met the family for a 'without prejudice' meeting to clarify conflicting statements from the Met and the IPCC (Independent Police Complaints Commission, now known as the Independent Office for Police Conduct). You could sense in the atmosphere that this case had the potential to have a massive impact.

One consequence of the 2011 riots was the emergence of this false narrative that all the violence was down to gangs – and that those gangs (according to the media) were predominantly black. A whole industry sprung up on the back of that, of people coming out of the woodwork and saying, 'I used to be a gang member; I could be the solution you're seeking.' This distorted the picture, addressing the whole spectrum of violence from one small perspective. Even now, with knife crime at its highest for 11 years, the violence involving gangs is less than 50 per cent.

The 'It's all gangs' narrative was regurgitated by the press and the police, but no one was getting to the real causes of the violence. From my experience and observations, a lot of it was down to inequality. People felt beleaguered with a lack of hope. The intervention and prevention programmes that stopped them from getting involved in criminality had suffered under the austerity programme, and violence had become the norm. Other factors included adverse childhood experiences in the home, sexual exploitation, toxic stress and a lack of resilience with which to resist it; high exclusion rates in schools, and a feeling among the young people that no one was listening to them.

Instead, what we heard repeatedly was a narrative presented by the likes of Boris Johnson and David Cameron, which no one in the Met was countering. It left a legacy of falsehood in its wake that wasn't corrected until 2016 by a report issued by the GLA (Greater London Authority), weeks before Johnson stood down as mayor. The report studied the causes of the riots in detail.

***

One of the people we encountered as part of REALLITY's work was a young man called Mario.

We first met Mario when I brought over Nicky Cruz and TRUCE in 2006. He was 18 at the time, and was in the Rochester Prison, where he featured as one of the testimonies on the outreach video I commissioned for the duration of the initiative. Over the next four years, our paths crossed on and off; we bumped into him again when REALLITY was delivering youth engagement work with the probation service in Waltham

Forest in 2008 and 2010, during which time Leah and Gerad struck up a friendship with him through wider Christian youth groups. From time to time Leah would tap into Mario's street knowledge to assist in the uptake of employment opportunities we offered to other young people. I was very pleased to attend Mario's baptism, because his journey from an at times chaotic lifestyle involved in crime to a positive person full of hope and expectation was so rewarding. This gave me great satisfaction, knowing of REALLITY's role in assisting him through the ups and downs.

Totally out of the blue, he and Leah sat me down in our living room and told me they were dating. This young man had been through the school of hard knocks and was an ex-offender. Now he was potentially my son-in-law. Now that he had become a Christian, it was clear that he wanted to turn his life around. He was totally committed to my daughter – and, likewise, she to him. All I could say was, 'God is the judge; he knows how sincere you are to your faith and my daughter.'

I think Leah was surprised that I didn't try to talk her out of it. I just sensed that if I'd gone in that direction, I would lose my daughter. It was abundantly clear she was in love with him – and still is, two beautiful children and eight years later.

Where I did put my foot down was when they wanted to get married immediately. I advised them to have a longer engagement time, and I suggested they give it a year, at least. Eventually they agreed on a date in the autumn of 2012, timed so that all my work on the Olympics would be over and done with before the wedding. More importantly, Gretl and I were grateful for the extra time fully to process the fact that our only daughter was engaged to be married to one of our outreach clients, and to consider how best we could support them.

***

As the Olympic Torch toured the country leading up to the Games, it gave each local authority the opportunity to showcase what made their area special. From then on, the Olympics began to feel like a national event. That momentum built up and fed into the opening ceremony. It was particularly touching for me to see Doreen Lawrence carrying the Olympic Torch into the stadium on the day the Games officially began. Danny Boyle did a brilliant job with the opening ceremony, bringing in so many aspects of British life and highlighting the people who were involved in pivotal moments of Britain's history. The closing ceremony had its moments too. It was very quirky, quintessentially British.

I saw the light touch of policing at the Olympics, where I observed officers dealing with people from different backgrounds and from all over the world, and doing so with a smile. I didn't hear of any incidents where heavy-handedness was involved.

I found myself remembering 6 July 2005, the day London won the bid. And at the same time, I remembered what happened the morning after. Our lives changed on 7/7, but it was clear that those ensuing years had been transformed into the positivity we saw at the Olympics – despite the riots that had occurred across London the year before.

Nevertheless, London 2012 was a great success and policing was no exception. It's in these large scale, country wide mobilizations I see the police service at its best. Invariably, the Met takes a leadership role in response to its national responsibilities, where we are the envy of the world, and many police departments across the world want to learn from us. The look and feel of policing changed during the summer of 2012, more like a police service than an occupying force, especially for minority ethnic communities around the country. After times like that, I wonder why we slip from that high standard?

The level of partnership we witnessed leading up to the Olympics – across ministries, across public sector organizations, across boroughs, communities being involved, especially young people – was phenomenal. I felt that there was nothing we couldn't achieve if we could just keep that mobilization alive; that galvanizing of communities, that sense of belonging. I saw the possibility of this country being at peace with itself and all the elements that make it up – and wanting to embrace them and not merely talk about 'tolerating' people, but rather accepting and cherishing their different backgrounds.

It saddens me to see how all the optimism we had during the Olympics has been eroded in the years that followed, especially in the run-up to Brexit, and afterwards. Attitudes that we'd thought had gone away clearly had just been lying dormant in some people's minds, and are now resurfacing, emboldened by the negative narrative of isolationism from Europe, creating barriers against some communities who do not feel welcome in this country. Look back at 2012 and compare it to today, and the difference in the public spirit is stark. How did we lose all the spark, vitality and beauty we had?

Leah's wedding that October offered pause for reflection as I prepared for retirement. It was a stage in my life that showed me what the past 30 years had really been all about, because in some way my children were the embodiment of my 30 years, especially Gerad, who was born in week 10 of my twenty-week foundation course at Hendon Police Training School. Seeing my children flourish and my family develop showed me that Gretl and I had done a good job. That's something weddings do, as you listen to the speeches and other verbal offerings of good will. Leah's wedding gave me a sense of peace and made me thankful for health and strength and for having that peace and joy in my spirit, underpinned by the foundation of our joint faith as a family.

In November 2014, a year after Leah's wedding, I received an honorary doctorate from my alma mater, the University of East London, for my contribution to policing. Again, it felt like a validation of all I had worked for during my years at the Met, as well as an excellent way to end the year. I enjoyed sharing the ceremony with Keir Starmer, who was also receiving the same award for his work as Director of Public Prosecutions, having just stood down with hidden political aspirations. He didn't keep us waiting for long, and was elected as an MP in 2015 and then became the leader of the Labour Party in 2020.

Honours and plaudits aside, I felt that there was still a lot of work left for me to do. The issues surrounding knife crime were building, and I didn't sense that I could just escape and live abroad six months of the year during the winter months. More and more, I would hear about acts of violence in London. Not only were they growing in number, the perpetrators and victims were getting younger and younger. It reminded me of how I'd joined the police in the first place. I felt I was being drawn back. This was compounded by the fact that I didn't want my grandchildren's generation living in fear as my children's generation had, with a key conclusion of mine that 'Families must steward their children positively or the streets will do so negatively.'

15

Back to life, back to Reallity

My career plan when I joined the Met had always been to retire once I'd made it through the full 30 years' service. By the time the Olympics were over, and the legacy documents written up, I was into my thirtieth year in the job. Thanks to all the work I'd done during (and after) the Games, I had accrued four months' worth of unspent annual leave and was able to have a less abrupt exit from the Met. It afforded me some time for reflection, and I even started to write this book.

I had my leaving party in the grand and majestic top floor function rooms of the Institute of Contemporary Arts on the Mall. I'm glad I videoed the excellent line-up of speakers including Sadiq Khan, who was now a minister in the shadow cabinet. He spoke about me in very complimentary terms, and was very funny and very engaging – although I thought his language was quite colourful for someone who doesn't normally swear. He couldn't even put it down to drink, as a devout Muslim! As he spoke, I was reminded of when he was my lawyer. We had kept in touch socially now and again, and he had asked my advice on policing, verbally and in print. Deputy Commissioner Craig Mackie served me my certificate of exemplary service after 30 years. We had some live music; Leee John performed with a handful of musicians, and I brought my trumpet along and played a duet of my old reggae favourite 'Police and Thieves' with Camara Fearon, my trumpet teacher, colleague and friend. What I liked most about my event was that the guests were mostly community people. I did have work colleagues there, but it was mainly a 'thank you' to the community for their support that would continue into retirement.

With the party over and the farewells said, I set about reviewing all the skills I had acquired during my time with the Met and assessing how useful they would be on Civvy Street. One big issue I had to come to terms with was that I felt I had become institutionalized, and I needed to de-programme myself.

I decided to go and find myself in the Amazon, of all places, and spent a month in Ecuador and Peru. My objective was to try to understand what had happened over the previous 30 years and how to make sense of it – and, more importantly, to keep a positive disposition. I wanted to understand how I'd contributed, and how (and in what form) that contribution could continue. I also wanted to see the Amazon rainforest before it got completely changed through deforestation and industrialization.

I was part of a team made up of people from all over the world, thrown together by a tour company called Dragoman. I enjoyed superb views on the night safaris, where the jungle seemed to glow in the dark and took on a life of its own, like the jungles in the film *Avatar*. The flora and fauna were amazing. When you turned your torch or your headlamp on and looked at the surroundings, you were blown away with the beauty of what you saw. It got a bit hair-raising and scary when you looked down and saw that you were in spitting distance of a tarantula.

I hadn't realized before how huge the Amazon was; this smaller river made the Thames look like a little tributary. There was a lot of oil industry work going on, and a whole economy operating alongside it. You would see petrol tankers on top of boats. It felt a bit like the English Channel.

Our guide said to us, 'Whatever you do, just trust me. If I tell you to stop, stop. If I say, "Don't stop", keep walking. If I say you can eat something, you can eat it. If I tell you to swim, swim; if I tell you to tread water, tread water.' We obeyed him totally.

Secretly I wished I'd been able to exact that sort of total obedience when I was in the hostile environment of the Met as a black supervisor!

The Amazon trip gave me some clarity regarding balance in my life post-Met and not just stopping dead in my tracks, because I could have ended up literally dead. The mortality rate for people who have been in high-octane jobs is very high if they suddenly stop doing those jobs. Stress is good, but if you have excessive stress in the environment in which you live and/or work, it can be quite toxic. In the Met, I lived off the stress, not just in dealing with the work but also with the culture within the organization, having to be strong in character and have that warrior spirit. But that warrior spirit does not lend itself to everyday life; if your routine changes, that warrior spirit can become a form of torment. The Amazon trip changed that in me. There was no need for me to be hyper vigilant, constantly on my guard all the time. I didn't have to worry about how people could undermine me – which was a daily reality when I was in the Met.

***

In retirement I still kept in touch with Sadiq and with Matthew Ryder QC, my anti-operation Helios legal team. Matthew and I are both long-suffering Arsenal supporters, so we were never short of things to discuss. Our team hadn't won anything of any real significance (well, they hadn't won the Premiership) since the early noughties, and we didn't know when it was going to happen next. Matthew would invite me to barbecues at his house, and these would turn out to be great networking opportunities. There were always people there who were in the arts, law and the media: people such as Baroness Lawrence and Chuka Umunna MP. Sadiq would often be there too.

In 2014, I went on a Mediterranean cruise covering Italy, Monte Carlo, Gibraltar and Portugal. Just before I went, Sadiq asked me to contribute to a publication he was editing for the Fabian Society, titled *Our London*. My former colleague Dal Babu and I co-wrote an essay titled 'Policing: bringing together the police and the public'. Dal and I called for more diversity within the Met, and for it to work in a more joined-up way with other public sector organizations. A few days before the cruise ended, Sadiq's people phoned and said he wanted me to be on the panel presenting at the launch of *Our London – The Capital Beyond 2015*. I was honoured to do that. The schedule was horribly tight, so I rushed from Southampton to Fishmongers' Hall in London in a cab to ensure I could take part in the panel.

Something struck me about *Our London* when I saw the finished product. To me, it felt like Chairman Mao's *Little Red Book*: *The Thoughts of Sadiq Khan*. It just seemed to have 'manifesto' written through it.

Sitting on that panel, I had the feeling that Sadiq was going for something. I didn't know what it was. I hadn't spoken to him in a while, but I found his whole demeanour had changed. He wasn't the easy-going guy I'd known for twelve or so years; he'd become sterner and had isolated himself. I knew he was doing a lot of work as a member of the shadow government, but *Our London* revealed someone with major political ambitions.

In January 2015 I went to see him at Portcullis House, to find out where he was coming from. Again, I sensed a change in his persona. When he was my lawyer, we had a real collaborative dynamic. That had all gone; he was much more cautious. '*Our London* document seems to me to be more than just a simple publication,' I said. Not surprisingly, he wouldn't comment, but I knew he was going for the London mayoral elections in May 2016.

My hunch proved to be on point when, soon after Labour lost the 2015 elections, Sadiq made it publicly known that he was running for mayor. I was not surprised when he asked me to be part of his campaign team, because of our working relations over the years. Having known Sadiq for as long as I have, I know when he's being open with me, and I just didn't feel that he was this time round. But I felt I owed him for all the help he'd given me in the past as my solicitor, so I agreed to speak at his campaign launch and to be included in marketing material.

In hindsight, I was probably politically naive to some extent by not asking some more critical questions and putting our arrangement in writing, but I was giving my mate the benefit of the doubt. I was involved in assisting some of his people because they tapped into my experience to build up the manifesto. I also did some intelligence work. Journalists were constantly trying to link Sadiq to certain individuals who had been found to be involved in terrorist activity. It was quite clear that the only link he had with them was that he was their solicitor, but the press tried to make mileage out of it. We wanted to ensure that there were no surprises. I had to tap into a couple of my contacts to find out how much intelligence the press had. I was always at the campaign office, but I always felt that at a certain level I was being shut out.

The campaign started in July. I spoke at the campaign launch in his home constituency, Tooting, in a church hall on Mitcham Lane very near to the estate where he grew up. I went to see him in his office in Tooting and sat down with him one to one. We had a good conversation; he was a lot more relaxed than previously, which I took as a good sign. I asked if he had any plans for me in his campaign. He said he wasn't going to make any decisions until after the election, but he valued my input and saw me as an advisor. He said that publicly at a meeting I set up for him with XLP, a charity that mentors young people in some of London's toughest estates. I knew XLP's founder Patrick Regan from the TRUCE days. Patrick agreed to meet Sadiq, even though he wasn't publicly endorsing any candidate. The meeting took place at XLP's office in All Hallows on the Wall in the city of London. Sadiq said in front of everyone at that meeting that I was his policy adviser on youth matters. Unfortunately, those words turned out to be hollow and worthless.

Sadiq's campaign received an unexpected boost on social media. Leading up to the 2016 London mayoral election, Donald Trump was on his own campaign to become US President, and was saying he would close the borders to Muslims if he was elected president. Sadiq jumped on this, pointing out that if he became mayor and Trump did what he said he would, he would not be able to go to America. This all happened on Twitter, and it launched Sadiq to another level, giving him the name recognition he craved and the campaign boost he desired. This was when I saw him becoming obsessed with his newfound public status, believing his fan mail. I saw this alter ego emerge that bordered on arrogance. 'Calm down, man,' I thought. 'The election isn't won yet!' I think he struggled to handle success. Nevertheless, I stayed loyal to the campaign and would send Sadiq encouraging text messages whenever the heat was on him.

On election night, we were asked to meet at a wine bar behind City Hall. I arrived there just after six o'clock. Everyone was in a celebratory mood. Sadiq didn't win on the first round, so he was up against the Tory candidate Zac Goldsmith for the second round. It was very late in the evening when we received word that he had definitely won, with 56.8 per cent of the vote against Goldsmith's 43.2 per cent.

When Sadiq finally came into the wine bar, there was euphoria. He gave me a big thumbs-up gesture and I gave one back. Sadiq's signing-in ceremony was scheduled to take place at Southwark Cathedral the following day. I was invited to that and I went, but I noticed that everyone in his team ignored me. This instantly reminded me of being shut out repeatedly by the

Met, during Operation Helios, when Sadiq defended me as my lawyer. It was a totally different scenario to the previous night, when everyone was cheering, hugging and shaking hands. All of a sudden, it was as if I didn't exist. I couldn't believe it. And in a cathedral, of all places! I wasn't surprised but I was disappointed.

I sent several emails and text messages to his senior advisor Jack Stenner, who I worked with throughout the campaign, but he never replied. His colleagues, who were copied into the messages, reassured me that he would make contact, but he didn't. At the same time, I was receiving emails and WhatsApp messages from around the world, congratulating me on 'my man' winning the election!

I then received an invitation to a private reception at the 'Mayor's Living Room' as it's called, at the top of City Hall. The campaign team were there, and so were members of Sadiq's family. I knew his wife and all his personal staff. I was totally blanked.

Sadiq went on stage and started to talk about his policies. When it came to policing, he announced that he was going to have an extra 600 armed police officers on the streets of London. Bevan Powell was with me. He had also been involved in Sadiq's campaign and had his eye on a seat on the GLA. I looked at Bevan and said, 'Did you hear that?'

'Yes,' he said.

'What does that say to you?' I asked.

'It's not what we advised him on,' Bevan replied.

We had advised him to take a more collaborative, holistic approach – and there he was, saying how many armed cops he was going to put on the streets! When did he decide this would deal with the crime problem London faced?

I never heard from him again.

***

Not working for Sadiq any more, however, meant that I was free to do community work without any political strings attached.

One of the youth pastors at my home church is a guy called Dez Brown. As a teenager, Dez was a product of his violent environment and ended up being jailed for manslaughter. He's turned his life around since then and is now the founder and CEO of Spark2Life (Sharing Positive and Relevant Keys to Life): a project that works with disaffected young people in prison, transitioning out of prison and in the community. They aim to help eradicate gang culture, knife crime and wider crime among young people – encouraging a positive social and behavioural lifestyle in those turning their back on a life of crime.

Dez asked me to do some gang engagement work, where I would go into a police station's custody office at the request of their gangs team, and see if any of the targeted young people they had in custody would benefit from being mentored by Spark2Life. Dez had lined up a retired American officer to do this at the custody suite at Waltham Forest, but he'd pulled out at the last minute. Spark2Life was now in danger of losing their funding if Dez couldn't find a replacement. I had the clearance, and I knew how to navigate through a lot of the policies and processes to make a good working relationship with the investigating officers in a shorter timeframe. A lot of them knew me from old anyway. I felt that God wanted me to do this, as a timely opportunity to work on relevant grassroots engagement with young people at a teachable moment in the custody office, where they are more open to being mentored into more positive lifestyles, and we are more willing to advocate for them than at any other stage in the justice and/or prison system.

Spark2Life was a welcome relief from politics; it was real hands-on work with real people. I was going back into police stations. The members of the gangs' teams at these police stations all knew me. The gangs' team would tell me they had someone who needed Spark2Life's help. I would then call the custody suite and speak to the investigating officer, then go in and speak to the young person. It meant I learned all about the changes that had happened in the Met since I'd left. I think a lot of the officers I interacted with through my work with Spark-2Life were surprised to see what I was doing. They knew I was a retired senior officer; they just couldn't understand why I wasn't on a beach somewhere. A couple of them actually asked me that. My reply was, 'We have a problem with violence and knives. Spark2Life have called on me to help.'

***

All throughout my career in the Met, I had to embrace and adopt new technology. For the most part, advances in technology have been of huge benefit to policing and crime detection. However, through my involvement with Spark2Life, I saw first-hand how one particular piece of new technology has done more harm than good.

The Gangs Matrix is an algorithm that was introduced by an American company called Accenture, as part of a predictive policing package adopted by the Met; equivalent analytical packages were adopted by GMP (Greater Manchester Police) and Nottingham Constabulary, covering cities with similar demographics to London. It has been in use in America for years; Accenture tried to get it into other countries in Europe, but they were rejected because it breached people's human rights. Accenture introduced the Gangs Matrix here in 2013. I went to the launch at City Hall, in my capacity as the chair of REAL-LITY. Boris Johnson was Mayor of London at the time; he and his 'gang czar', Ray Lewis, introduced it to us. Almost immediately, it set off alarm bells for me. Consequently, when I was working on the manifesto of Sadiq Khan's campaign to become

London mayor, I flagged up the issue and it was included, with the intention of carrying out a review once he was elected. If I had been one of his advisors post-election, I would have ensured it was carried out sooner, in months, rather than later in years.

The algorithm took people's past histories into account: their associates, and what was on the Met's Criminal Intelligence System (CIS) about that individual. There appeared to be no independent oversight of the system. No one would check independently on the quality of the data going into it, and it was almost impossible to remove data from it. As a result of this, people had markers on them from this intelligence system, saying they might be involved in weapons, drugs, violence – but to get that marker off the system was almost impossible. I remember one person who used to get stopped because of a weapons marker on his car. In the end, he had to sell it because he was being stopped all the time, just going about his lawful business. Being stopped and searched by regular officers is bad enough, let alone a 'hard stop' with armed officers pointing guns at you!

The Matrix took into account a person's past history, and some of that information came from social media. So people could say things on Instagram or Facebook with a lot of bravado, and it would be used against them. The algorithm had also been found to lack cultural accuracy, because it was based on the Met's CIS, which was proven to be very generalized and subjective, making many assumptions and using stereotypes.

When I started working for Spark2Life in the custody suites, I realized very quickly that there were some real problems with the Matrix. After a year and a half of doing that work, I had spoken to over 50 clients, and out of 25 investigating officers, only one came back to me and said, 'I don't think this person should be in the Matrix.' I asked why, and he said, 'First, that client is not known to be in a gang. He knows people who are, because he went to school with some of them and they live in the same area. But he has learning difficulties and if he trusts someone, he can be very easily led. His offence is being in the wrong place at the wrong time.' It was clear that this young man had been put on the Matrix because of his associates, because of the way in which the information is collated in the CIS. This was not an isolated case and clearly showed racism, so it is not surprising that over 70 per cent of gangs on the algorithm were of African-Caribbean origins and white European ones were conspicuous by their absence. This was another example of a systemic failure within the Met, that I have been challenging for over 20 years since the Macpherson Inquiry. In my view, the Matrix was another form of institutional racism – this time by algorithm. There were countless other examples of the Matrix stigmatizing other people along racial lines.

In October 2017, following concerns raised by Amnesty International, Stop Watch and Manchester Metropolitan University, the Information Commissioner's Office launched an investigation into the Met's use of the Gangs Matrix. The results of the investigation were published in 2018, and they resonated with the review carried out by the Mayor's Office for Policing and Crime (MOPAC). All of them found that the Met's use of the Matrix had led to 'multiple and serious breaches of data protection laws'.

I made my personal submission through my final report on the Spark2life Custody Office project to MOPAC, highlighting the deliberate racialization of gangs and how white gangs were conspicuous by their absence on the Matrix. Other aspects of policing by algorithms, including AI (Artificial Intelligence), have given me a great deal of concern, which I have taken forward through some preliminary research on FRS (Facial Recognition Systems) in partnership with the Royal Society of Arts. I have also worked with Tortoise Media on this critical issue, as well as separately taking part in a German-produced film in 2017 called *Pre-Crime*. My consistent request to policing authority figures involved in the Matrix and FRS is the critical need for independent oversight in all of these systems to prevent legal loopholes being exploited, because the legislation is not keeping pace with technology. Additionally, the CIS (Criminal Intelligence System) on which these systems are based must not be biased, due to stereotypes or assumptions, against any colour or class of people who are already regularly on the receiving end of a disproportionate use of heavy-handed police enforcement. By incorporating these checks and balances into these technologies, they are less likely to be racialized.

***

I often joke that the easiest way to cut your Christmas card list by 99 per cent is to join the police. I'm very grateful to my 'one per cent' – the friends and family who stayed loyal and supportive when many deserted me after my decision to become a cop. Initially, I had Gretl, my parents and my sister, but as my family has grown, my children and grandchildren have become a great source of loving support. It's great having a few other people who were there for me as well. They may not have all agreed with my decision at first, but they have always been supportive close friends for 50 years. There's Leee John, of course, and Omar Atie, who set me up on that blind date with Gretl all those years ago in 1976. And Junior Douglas, another friend from Highbury Grove School. Junior and I played trumpet together and got on well, even though I used to make fun of him for being an Elton John and Rod Stewart fan!

Leee's mum, Jessie Stephens MBE, was my main support from the beginning, encouraging me to join the Met and understanding the need for a police service to reflect London. She stood up for me when my father understandably opposed me joining the Met, as well as building my conviction to stick at it when so many other people were against me and openly hostile at times.

The Right Reverend Rose Hudson-Wilkin MBE was a real asset to me when I was at Hackney, especially during the TRUCE outreach project. She was another person who modelled faith in action in a proactive way. She was always available to be the community representative on numerous critical matters. When I left Hackney to work on the Olympics, Rose asked me to be a referee for a few jobs she was applying for. I was more than happy to oblige. Shortly after I'd supplied the references, Rose called again.

'Leroy,' she said, 'there's one more job I'd like you to give me a reference for.'

'Sure,' I said. 'What is it?'

Rose explained that she had been shortlisted for the role of Chaplain to the Speaker of the House of Commons. 'That is your job,' I said. I wrote the greatest reference I have ever written. It was a real joy doing it – and an even bigger joy when she got the job. I've learned a lot from Rose, especially about how faith builds resilience. She has made history again by her appointment as the first black female Anglican bishop in 2019, which is Dover's gain and London's loss.

Another faith leader I've learned a great deal from is Reverend Joel Edwards, the former General Secretary of the Evangelical Alliance. I've known Joel for over 20 years, especially when I was doing work on Street Pastors; the Evangelical Alliance worked with the Ascension Trust. Joel continued to be a support to me when he moved from the Evangelical Alliance to the Micah Challenge. Dez Brown of Spark2life has also been one of my champions.

It is widely accepted that a person is only as good as the people they surround themselves with and the friends they choose, especially when they are in strong occupational cultures like the Met. Therefore having a mentor like Robin Merrett in critical stages of my career cannot be over-estimated. The fact that they have a similar influence on me in retirement speaks volumes. Another mentor with a similar impact on me through his wise counsel from outside the Met was Harry Fletcher, who unexpectedly died from natural causes at the beginning of 2020. He was a senior probation officer who was one of the public faces of the Probation Service, when he was Assistant General Secretary for the National Association of Probation Officers and even in his well-respected consultancy role in retirement. When his partner, Kate, and sons – William and George – asked me to be one of his pall bearers, I was profoundly humbled. Rest in peace, Harry.

These 'one per centers' helped keep my feet firmly on the ground. Although not all of them embraced my career choice at first, they stuck with me and said, 'Let's see how it goes.' One can get so immersed in police culture that you assimilate into it without thinking, but I always maintained very clearly that I'm a black man who happens to be a cop. Having those key friends kept me grounded; I never felt that I was alone. As I went up through the ranks, they grew prouder and prouder of me, always happy to tell people I was a senior cop doing work of prominence around race, equality and justice. They may have doubted my decision at first, but now they more or less agree that I made the right choice, in a similar way to my Dad's unforeseen declaration the day I was awarded my MBE in 2000.

I am happy that I never stopped the focus on young people – not even in retirement. This is not just a week, a month, a year or a decade; it's a lifetime vocation until we get this knife crime issue sorted. The inequalities and injustices in society are building up, and they will only reverse when we go back to the basic principles of respect, dignity and love for each other.

Also we have to push back on 'decisions by decibels', with ill-conceived soundbites that cause division instead of unity, like those that come from your Johnsons and your Trumps – hogging the conversation with populist right wing isolationist narratives that create suspicion and fear.

I'm glad we went through all the sacrifices we did to get the BPA up and running over 25 years ago. Many thanks to Deborah Thomas and Tracy Gittens – aka Washington – for their long term commitment in keeping the Met BPA office running for over 20 years in support of the chairs, executive committee and wider membership, in addition to coordinating the numerous outreach programmes and work with the Voyage Youth family.

Several BPA members have shone brightly, rising to prominence in various spheres: members such as Bevan Powell MBE, a former Met BPA chair. Like me he was fully committed to Voyage Youth and was instrumental in developing the BTech level ll Young Leaders for Safer Cities programme, to assist our young people in empowering themselves and to reduce the risk of others taking advantage of their vulnerabilities. Maybe I'm being too utopian, but I don't want my grandchildren to grow up in fear and with these injustices and inequalities affecting them, in a similar way my children's generation have had to.

One of the most humble and unassuming members who led the BPA at the 1994 launch for a year and has been a long-term mentor of mine is Ron Hope. He was one of the first black chief superintendents in late 1999 with Mike Fuller – another chair – and they were both part of the first tranche of new borough commander roles shortly afterwards. Mike went on to become the first black chief constable in 2004, in the county of Kent.

***

One Bible character I identified heavily with during my years in the Metropolitan Police is Joseph of Arimathea, who is mentioned in all the Gospels, especially in Luke 23:50-56. He was on a journey of discipleship, doing his best to be 'a good and upright man of substance', and I could see many parallels between Joseph's journey and mine. He crossed cultural barriers by burying Jesus in his family tomb and not treating him like an outcast. I had to do that many times in my career, most notably when I was working with the So Solid Crew and gave character evidence at Megaman's three trials for conspiracy to murder. Joseph plucked up courage, was bold, and did not play it safe or stay in his comfort zone. That was the story of my life since joining the Met. He did not agree with the Sanhedrin and stood up for Jesus, in a similar way that I had to in the uproar that erupted when the TRUCE team came to Hackney. Lastly, Joseph gave of himself by standing up for righteousness. Again, that was an ongoing theme in my career in policing and still is in retirement.

I have no regrets, but I am glad that my 30 years in the Met are over. All throughout my career, I experienced some form or other of culture shock brought about by the internal hostile environment in the Met. I knew I had to go through with it to the very end, but when I retired in 2013, I felt a sense of freedom. The testosterone-driven macho environment, intolerant to difference and demanding total conformity to the norms and values of the culture, is something I have not missed for a second. Despite the massive toll it took on my life, I have no regrets, because as I look back, it all makes sense.

Appendix

Order of ranks of officers in the Metropolitan Police
(Listed in order of seniority – lowest first)

Constable
Sergeant
Inspector
Chief Inspector
Superintendent
Chief Superintendent
Commander
Deputy Assistant Commissioner
Deputy Commissioner
Commissioner

(Source: Police National Legal Database)

Timeline for significant events

1952	My father settles in London from Jamaica
1954	My mother joins him from Jamaica
1957	I was born in Islington
1962	Moved to Jamaica with my mother and sister
1966	Moved back to London
1968	Attended Highbury Grove School
1973	Attended Hackney College
June 1980	Graduated with a BSC in Applied Biology
July 1980	Joined the Royal Free
Summer 1982	Applied to join the Met
Autumn 1982	My father was beaten up by Hornsey Division police officers
June 1983	I started police foundation training at Hendon
November 1983	First posting as a Constable to Islington Division station
May 1985	Joined the newly formed Crime Desk
August 1986	Set up the Divisional Intelligence and Information Unit at Kings Cross station
November 1988	Promoted to sergeant at Edmonton station
1989	Before the civil action case is heard at court, my father is compensated by the Met for unlawful arrest and excessive force used in the 1982 beating
1990	Met Bristol seminars on the disproportionate resignations of black and minority ethnic officers
1991	Start of the Bristol Reunions
April 1993	Founder member meeting of the Black Police Association (BPA)
April 1993	Stephen Lawrence racially murdered
September 1994	Launch of the Met BPA; elected Treasurer
1996	Inaugural meeting of the National Communication Network (NCN)
September 1997	Promoted to Inspector at Enfield station

Timeline for significant events

1998	Secured BPA Charitable Trust charity status
1998	Oral evidence given to the Macpherson Inquiry, published in February 1999
November 1998	Elected first Chairperson of the National BPA
January 1999	Intake Manager at Hendon Training School
May 1999	Launch of the Manchester BPA
November 1999	Launch of the National BPA
January 2000	Received an MBE in the Queen's New Year Honours list
July 2000	Inspector of Partnership at Westminster Borough and Project Manager for the Paddington Community Project
October 2000	Chairperson of the Met BPA until October 2004, including the Charitable Trust
November 2000	Murder of Damilola Taylor – Cultural Resource Unit formed
January 2001	Allegations against Ali Dizaei – Operation Helios
May 2001	Chief Inspector Partnership at Westminster Borough
June 2001	Criminal allegation made – Operation Helios
2003	Recruitment ban by the Met BPA until there was a public inquiry
2004	Morris Inquiry launched 31 January – report published 14 December
September 2004	Superintendent Operations and Partnership at Hackney Borough
July 2006	TRUCE outreach programme
November 2007	Joined the 2012 Olympic Security Team that was finally known as the Olympic Policing Coordination Team (OPCT)
November 2007	Set up REALLITY as a Community Interest Company
August 2011	Tottenham disorders that led to riots across England
November 2011	Second term as Chairperson of the BPA Charitable Trust – renamed Voyage Youth in 2016 and patronized by Neville Lawrence since 2001
July 2013	Retired from the Met

WE HAVE A VISION OF A WORLD IN WHICH EVERYONE IS TRANSFORMED BY CHRISTIAN KNOWLEDGE

As well as being an award-winning publisher, SPCK is the oldest Anglican mission agency in the world.

Our mission is to lead the way in creating books and resources that help everyone to make sense of faith.

Will you partner with us to put good books into the hands of prisoners, great assemblies in front of schoolchildren and reach out to people who have not yet been transformed by the Christian faith?

To donate, please visit www.spckpublishing.co.uk/donate or call our friendly fundraising team on 020 7592 3900.